the ordinary person's guide to empire

arundhati roy

the ordinary person's guide to empire

HARPER PERENNIAL

Harper Perennial
An Imprint of HarperCollins*Publishers*
77–85 Fulham Palace Road,
Hammersmith, London W6 8JB

www.harpercollins.co.uk/harperperennial

This edition published by Harper Perennial 2004
First published in Great Britain by Flamingo 2004
5

A catalogue record for this book is available from the British Library

ISBN 0 00 718163 9

Set in Meridien
Typeset by Rowland Phototypesetting Limited,
Bury St Edmunds, Suffolk

Printed and bound in Great Britain by
Clays Ltd, St Ives plc

contents

ahimsa
(non-violent resistance)

ahimsa
(non-violent resistance)

While the rest of us are mesmerized by talk of war and terrorism and wars against terror, in the state of Madhya Pradesh in central India, a little life-raft has set sail into the wind. On a pavement in Bhopal, in an area called Tin Shed, a small group of people has embarked on a journey of faith and hope. There's nothing new in what they're doing. What's new is the climate in which they're doing it.

Today is the twenty-ninth day of the indefinite hunger strike by four activists of the Narmada Bachao Andolan (NBA), the Save the Narmada Movement.[1] They have fasted two days longer than Gandhi did on any of his fasts during the freedom struggle. Their demands are more modest than his ever were. They are protesting against the Madhya Pradesh government's forcible eviction of more than one thousand Adivasi (indigenous) families to make way for the Maan Dam. All they're asking is that the government of Madhya Pradesh implement its own policy of providing land to those being displaced by the Maan Dam.

There's no controversy here. The dam has been built. The displaced people must be resettled before the reservoir fills up in the monsoon and submerges their villages. The four activists on fast are Vinod Patwa, who was one of the one hundred and fourteen thousand people displaced in 1990 by the Bargi Dam (which now, twelve years later, irrigates less land than it submerged); Mangat Verma, who will be displaced by the Maheshwar Dam if it is ever completed; Chittaroopa Palit, who has worked with the NBA for almost fifteen years; and twenty-two-year-old Ram Kunwar, the youngest and frailest of the activists. Hers is the first village that will be submerged when the waters rise in the Maan reservoir. In the weeks since she began her fast, Ram Kunwar has lost twenty pounds – almost one-quarter of her original body weight.

Unlike the other large dams such as the Sardar Sarovar, Maheshwar and Indira Sagar, where the resettlement of hundreds of thousands of displaced people is simply not possible (except on paper, in court documents), in the case of Maan the total number of displaced people is about six thousand. People have even identified land that is available and could be bought and allotted to them by the government. And yet the government refuses. Instead it's busy distributing paltry cash compensation, which is illegal and violates its own policy. It says quite openly that if it were to give in to the demands of the Maan 'oustees' (that is, if it implemented its own policy), it would set a precedent for the hundreds of thousands of people, most of them Dalits (untouchables) and Adivasis, who are slated to be submerged (without rehabilitation) by the twenty-nine other big dams planned in the Narmada valley. And the state government's commitment to these projects remains absolute, regardless of the social and environmental costs.

As Vinod, Mangat, Chittaroopa, and Ram Kunwar gradually weaken, as their systems close down and the risk of irreversible organ failure and sudden death sets in, no government official has bothered to even pay them a visit.

Let me tell you a secret – it's not all unwavering resolve and steely determination on the burning pavement under the pitiless sun at Tin Shed. The jokes about slimming and weight loss are becoming a little poignant now. There are tears of anger and frustration. There is trepidation and real fear. But underneath all that, there's pure grit.

What will happen to them? Will they just go down in the ledgers as 'the price of progress'? That phrase cleverly frames the whole argument as one between those who are pro-development versus those who are anti-development – and suggests the inevitability of the choice you have to make: pro-development, what else? It slyly suggests that movements like the NBA are antiquated and absurdly anti-electricity or anti-irrigation. This of course is nonsense.

The NBA believes that Big Dams are obsolete. It believes there are more democratic, more local, more economically viable and environmentally sustainable ways of generating electricity and managing water systems. It is demanding *more* modernity, not less. It is demanding *more* democracy, not less. And look at what's happening instead.

Even at the height of the war rhetoric, even as India and Pakistan threatened each other with nuclear annihilation, the question of reneging on the Indus Waters Treaty between the two countries did not arise.[2] Yet in Madhya Pradesh, the police and administration entered Adivasi villages with bulldozers. They sealed hand pumps, demolished school buildings, and clear-felled trees in order to force people from their homes. They *sealed* hand pumps. And so, the indefinite hunger strike.

Any government's condemnation of terrorism is only credible if it shows itself to be responsive to persistent, reasonable, closely argued, non-violent dissent. And yet, what's happening is just the opposite. The world over, non-violent resistance movements are being crushed and broken. If we do not respect and honour them, by default we privilege those who turn to violent means.

Across the world, when governments and the media lavish all their time, attention, funds, research, space, sophistication, and seriousness on war talk and terrorism, then the message that goes out is disturbing and dangerous: If you seek to air and redress a public grievance, violence is more effective than non-violence. Unfortunately, if peaceful change is not given a chance, then violent change becomes inevitable. That violence will be (and already is) random, ugly and unpredictable. What's happening in Kashmir, the north-eastern states of India, and Andhra Pradesh is all part of this process.

Right now the NBA is not just fighting big dams. It's fighting for the survival of India's greatest gift to the world: non-violent resistance. You could call it the Ahimsa Bachao Andolan (ahimsa means 'non-violent resistance'), or the Save Non-violence Movement. Over the years our government has shown nothing but contempt for the people of the Narmada valley. Contempt for their argument. Contempt for their movement.

In the twenty-first century the connection between religious fundamentalism, nuclear nationalism, and the pauperization of whole populations because of corporate globalization is becoming impossible to ignore. While the Madhya Pradesh government has categorically said it has no land for the rehabilitation of displaced people, reports say that it is preparing the ground (pardon the pun) to make huge tracts of land available for corporate agriculture. This in turn will set off another cycle of displacement and impoverishment.

Can we prevail on Digvijay Singh – the secular, 'green' chief minister of Madhya Pradesh – to substitute some of his public relations with a *real* change in policy? If he did, he would go down in history as a man of vision and true political courage. If the Congress Party wishes to be taken seriously as an alternative to the destructive right-wing religious fundamentalists who have brought us to the threshold of ruin, it will have to do more than condemn communalism and participate in empty nationalist rhetoric. It will have to do some real work and some real listening to the people it claims to represent.

As for the rest of us, concerned citizens, peace activists, and the like – it's not enough to sing songs about giving peace a chance. Doing everything we can to support movements like the Narmada Bachao

Andolan is *how* we give peace a chance. *This* is the real war against terror.

Go to Bhopal. Just ask for Tin Shed.[3]

come september

come september

Writers imagine that they cull stories from the world. I'm beginning to believe that vanity makes them think so. That it's actually the other way around. Stories cull writers from the world. Stories reveal themselves to us. The public narrative, the private narrative – they colonize us. They commission us. They insist on being told. Fiction and non-fiction are only different techniques of storytelling. For reasons I do not fully understand, fiction dances out of me. Non-fiction is wrenched out by the aching, broken world I wake up to every morning.

The theme of much of what I write, fiction as well as non-fiction, is the relationship between power and powerlessness and the endless, circular conflict they're engaged in. John Berger, that most wonderful writer, once wrote:

> Never again will a single story be told as though it's the only one.[1]

There can never be a single story. There are only ways of seeing. So when I tell a story, I tell it not as an ideologue who wants to pit one absolutist ideology against another, but as a storyteller who wants to share her way of seeing. Though it might appear otherwise, my writing is not really about nations and histories, it's about power. About the paranoia and ruthlessness of power. About the physics of power. I believe that the accumulation of vast unfettered power by a state or a country, a corporation or an institution – or even an individual, a spouse, friend, or sibling – regardless of ideology, results in excesses such as the ones I will recount here.

Living as I do, as millions of us do, in the shadow of the nuclear holocaust that the governments of India and Pakistan keep promising their brainwashed citizenry, and in the global neighbourhood of the War Against Terror (what President Bush rather biblically calls 'the task that does not end'), I find myself thinking a great deal about the relationship between citizens and the state.[2]

In India, those of us who have expressed views on nuclear bombs, Big Dams, corporate globalization, and the rising threat of communal Hindu fascism – views that are at variance with the Indian government's – are branded 'anti-national'. While this accusation does not fill me with indignation, it's not an accurate description of what I do or how I think. An anti-national is a person who is against her own nation and, by inference, is pro some other one. But it isn't necessary to be anti-national to be deeply suspicious of all nationalism, to be anti-national*ism*. Nationalism of one kind or another was the cause of most of the genocide of the twentieth century. Flags are bits of coloured cloth that governments use first to shrink-wrap people's minds and then as ceremonial shrouds to bury the dead. When independent, thinking people (and here I do not include the corporate media) begin to rally under flags, when writers, painters, musicians, film-makers suspend their judgement and blindly yoke their art to the service of the nation, it's time for all of us to sit up and worry. In India we saw it happen soon after the nuclear tests in 1998 and during the Kargil War against Pakistan in 1999. In the US we saw it during the Gulf War and we see it now, during the War Against Terror. That blizzard of made-in-China American flags.[3]

Recently, those who have criticized the actions of the US government (myself included) have been called 'anti-American'. Anti-Americanism is in the process of being consecrated into an ideology.

The term 'anti-American' is usually used by the American establishment to discredit and – not falsely, but shall we say inaccurately – define its critics. Once someone is branded anti-American, the chances are that he or she will be judged before they're heard and the argument will be lost in the welter of bruised national pride.

What does the term 'anti-American' *mean*? Does it mean you're anti-jazz? Or that you're opposed to free speech? That you don't delight in Toni Morrison or John Updike? That you have a quarrel with giant sequoias? Does it mean you don't admire the hundreds of thousands of American citizens who marched against nuclear weapons, or the thousands of war resisters who forced their government to withdraw from Vietnam? Does it mean that you hate all Americans?

This sly conflation of America's culture, music, literature, the breathtaking physical beauty of the land, the ordinary pleasures of ordinary people with criticism of the US government's foreign policy (about which, thanks to America's 'free press', sadly, most Americans know very little) is a deliberate and extremely effective strategy. It's like a retreating army taking cover in a heavily populated city, hoping that the prospect of hitting civilian targets will deter enemy fire.

There are many Americans who would be mortified to be associated with their government's policies. The most scholarly, scathing, incisive, hilarious critiques of the hypocrisy and the contradictions in US government policy come from American citizens. When the rest of the world wants to know what the US government is up to, we turn to Noam Chomsky, Edward Said, Howard Zinn, Ed Herman, Amy Goodman, Michael Albert, Chalmers Johnson, William Blum, and Anthony Arnove to tell us what's really going on. Similarly, in India, not hundreds, but millions of us would be ashamed and offended if we were in any way implicated with the present Indian government's fascist policies which, apart from the perpetration of state terrorism in the valley of Kashmir (in the name of fighting terrorism), have also turned a blind eye to the recent state-supervised pogrom against Muslims in Gujarat.[4] It would be absurd to think that those who criticize the Indian government are 'anti-Indian' – although the government itself never hesitates to take that line. It is dangerous to cede to the Indian government or the American government, or *anyone* for that matter, the right to define what 'India' or 'America' are, or ought to be.

To call someone anti-American, indeed, to *be* anti-American (or for that matter anti-Indian, or anti-Timbuktuan) is not just racist, it's a failure of the imagination. An inability to see the world in terms other than those that the establishment has set out for you: If you're not a Bushie, you're a Taliban. If you don't love us, you hate us. If you're not Good, you're Evil. If you're not with us, you're with the terrorists.

Last year, like many others, I too made the mistake of scoffing at this post-September 11th rhetoric, dismissing it as foolish and arrogant. I've realized that it's not foolish at all. It's actually a canny recruitment drive for a misconceived, dangerous war. Every day I'm taken aback at how many people believe that opposing the war in Afghanistan amounts to supporting terrorism, or voting for the Taliban. Now that the initial aim of the war – capturing Osama bin Laden (dead or alive) – seems to have run into bad weather, the goalposts have been moved.[5] It's being made out that the whole point of the war was to topple the Taliban regime and liberate Afghan women from their burqas. We're being asked to believe that the US marines are actually on a feminist mission. (If so, will their next stop be America's military ally Saudi Arabia?) Think of it this way: In India there are some pretty reprehensible social practices, against 'untouchables', against Christians and Muslims, against women. Pakistan and Bangladesh have even worse ways of dealing with minority communities and women. Should they be bombed? Should Delhi, Islamabad, and Dhaka be destroyed? Is it possible to bomb bigotry out of India? Can we bomb our way to a feminist paradise? Is that how women won the vote in the United States? Or how slavery was abolished? Can we win redress for the genocide of the millions of Native Americans upon whose corpses the United States was founded by bombing Santa Fe? None of us need anniversaries to remind us of what we cannot forget. So it is no more than coincidence that I happen to be here, on American soil, in September – this month of dreadful anniversaries. Uppermost in everybody's mind of course, particularly here in America, is the horror of what has come to be known as '9/11'. Three thousand civilians lost their lives in that lethal terrorist strike.[6] The grief is still deep. The rage still sharp. The tears have not dried. And a strange, deadly war is raging around the world. Yet each person who has lost a loved one surely knows secretly, deeply, that no war, no act of revenge, no daisy-cutters dropped on someone else's loved ones or someone else's children will blunt the edges of their pain or bring their own loved ones back. War cannot avenge those who have died. War is only a brutal desecration of their memory.

To fuel yet another war – this time against Iraq – by cynically manipulating people's grief, by packaging it for TV specials sponsored by corporations selling detergent or running shoes, is to cheapen and devalue grief, to drain it of meaning. What we are seeing now is a vulgar display of the *business* of grief, the commerce of grief, the pillaging of even the most private human feelings for political purpose. It is a terrible, violent thing for a state to do to its people.

It's not a clever enough subject to speak of from a public platform, but what I would really love to talk to you about is loss. Loss and losing. Grief, failure, brokenness, numbness, uncertainty, fear, the death of feeling, the death of dreaming. The absolute, relentless, endless, habitual unfairness of the world. What does loss mean to individuals? What does it mean to whole cultures, whole peoples who have learned to live with it as a constant companion?

Since it is September 11th that we're talking about, perhaps it's in the fitness of things that we remember what that date means, not only to those who lost their loved ones in America last year, but to those in other parts of the world to whom that date has long held significance. This historical dredging is not offered as an accusation or a provocation. But just to share the grief of history. To thin the mist a little. To say to the citizens of America, in the gentlest, most human way: Welcome to the World.

Twenty-nine years ago, in Chile, on the 11th of September 1973, General Pinochet overthrew the democratically elected government of Salvador Allende in a CIA-backed coup. 'I don't see why we need to stand by and watch a country go Communist due to the irresponsibility of its own people,' said Henry Kissinger, Nobel Peace Laureate, then President Nixon's National Security Adviser.[7]

After the coup President Allende was found dead inside the presidential palace. Whether he was killed or whether he killed himself, we'll never know. In the regime of terror that ensued, thousands of people were killed. Many more simply 'disappeared'. Firing squads conducted public executions. Concentration camps and torture chambers were opened across the country. The dead were buried in mine shafts and unmarked graves. For more than sixteen years the people of Chile lived in dread of the midnight knock, of routine disappearances, of sudden arrest and torture.[8]

In 2000, following the 1998 arrest of General Pinochet in Britain, thousands of secret documents were declassified by the US government.[9] They contain unequivocal evidence of the CIA's involvement in the coup as well as the fact that the US government had detailed information about the situation in Chile during General Pinochet's reign. Yet Kissinger assured the general of his support: 'In the United States, as you know, we are sympathetic with what you are trying to do,' he said. 'We wish your government well.'[10]

Those of us who have only ever known life in a democracy, however flawed, would find it hard to imagine what living in a dictatorship and enduring the absolute loss of freedom really means. It isn't just those who Pinochet murdered, but the lives he stole from the living that must be accounted for too.

Sadly, Chile was not the only country in South America to be singled out for the US government's attentions. Guatemala, Costa Rica, Ecuador, Brazil, Peru, the Dominican Republic, Bolivia, Nicaragua, Honduras, Panama, El Salvador, Peru, Mexico, and Colombia: they've all been the playground for covert – and overt – operations by the CIA.[11] Hundreds of thousands of Latin Americans have been killed, tortured, or have simply disappeared under the despotic regimes and tin-pot dictators, drug runners, and arms dealers that were propped up in their countries. (Many of them learned their craft in the infamous US-government-funded School of Americas in Fort Benning, Georgia, which has produced sixty thousand graduates.)[12] If this were not humiliation enough, the people of South America have had to bear the cross of being branded as a people who are incapable of democracy – as if coups and massacres are somehow encrypted in their genes.

This list does not of course include countries in Africa or Asia that suffered US military interventions –

Somalia, Vietnam, Korea, Indonesia, Laos, and Cambodia.[13] For how many Septembers for decades together have millions of Asian people been bombed, burned, and slaughtered? How many Septembers have gone by since August 1945, when hundreds of thousands of ordinary Japanese people were obliterated by the nuclear strikes in Hiroshima and Nagasaki? For how many Septembers have the thousands who had the misfortune of surviving those strikes endured the living hell that was visited on them, their unborn children, their children's children, on the earth, the sky, the wind, the water, and all the creatures that swim and walk and crawl and fly? Not far from here, in Albuquerque, is the National Atomic Museum, where Fat Man and Little Boy (the affectionate nicknames for the bombs that were dropped on Hiroshima and Nagasaki) were available as souvenir earrings. Funky young people wore them. A massacre dangling in each ear. But I am straying from my theme. It's September that we're talking about, not August.

September 11th has a tragic resonance in the Middle East too. On the 11th of September 1922, ignoring Arab outrage, the British government proclaimed a mandate in Palestine, a follow-up to the 1917 Balfour Declaration, which imperial Britain issued with its army massed outside the gates of the city of Gaza.[14] The Balfour Declaration promised European Zionists 'a national home for Jewish people'.[15] (At the time, the empire on which the sun never set was free to snatch and bequeath national homes like the school bully distributes marbles.) Two years after the declaration, Lord Arthur James Balfour, the British foreign secretary, said:

> *In Palestine we do not propose even to go through the form of consulting the wishes of the present inhabitants of the country . . . Zionism, be it right or wrong, good or bad, is rooted in age-long tradition, in present needs, in future hopes, of far profounder import than the desires and prejudices of the 700,000 Arabs who now inhabit that ancient land.*[16]

How carelessly imperial power decreed whose needs were profound and whose were not. How carelessly it vivisected ancient civilizations. Palestine and Kashmir are imperial Britain's festering, blood-drenched gifts to the modern world. Both are fault lines in the raging international conflicts of today.

In 1937 Winston Churchill said of the Palestinians:

> *I do not agree that the dog in a manger has the final right to the manger, even though he may have lain there for a very long time. I do not admit that right. I do not admit, for instance, that a*

great wrong has been done to the Red Indians of
America, or the black people of Australia. I do not
admit that a wrong has been done to these people
by the fact that a stronger race, a higher grade
race, a more wordly-wise race, to put it that way,
has come in and taken their place.[17]

That set the trend for the Israeli state's attitude toward
Palestinians. In 1969, Israeli Prime Minister Golda
Meir said, 'Palestinians do not exist.' Her predecessor,
Prime Minister Levi Eshkol, said, 'Where are Palestinians? When I came here [to Palestine] there were
250,000 non-Jews, mainly Arabs and Bedouins. It was
desert, more than underdeveloped. Nothing.' Prime
Minister Menachem Begin called Palestinians 'two-
legged beasts'. Prime Minister Yitzhak Shamir called
them '"grasshoppers" who could be crushed'.[18] This
is the language of heads of state, not the words of
ordinary people. In 1947, the UN formally partitioned
Palestine and allotted 55 per cent of Palestine's land
to the Zionists. Within a year they had captured more
than 76 per cent.[19] On 14 May 1948 the State of
Israel was declared. Minutes after the declaration, the
United States recognized Israel. The West Bank was
annexed by Jordan. The Gaza Strip came under the
military control of Egypt.[20] Formally, Palestine ceased
to exist except in the minds and hearts of the hundreds of thousands of Palestinian people who became
refugees.

In the summer of 1967, Israel occupied the West Bank and the Gaza Strip. Settlers were offered state subsidies and development aid to move into the occupied territories. Almost every day more Palestinian families are forced off their lands and driven into refugee camps. Palestinians who continue to live in Israel do not have the same rights as Israelis and live as second-class citizens in their former homeland.[21]

Over the decades there have been uprisings, wars, *intifadas*. Thousands have lost their lives.[22] Accords and treaties have been signed. Cease-fires declared and violated. But the bloodshed doesn't end. Palestine still remains illegally occupied. Its people live in inhuman conditions, in virtual Bantustans, where they are subjected to collective punishments and twenty-four-hour curfews, where they are humiliated and brutalized on a daily basis. They never know when their homes will be demolished, when their children will be shot, when their precious trees will be cut down, when their roads will be closed, when they will be allowed to walk down to the market to buy food and medicine. And when they will not. They live with no semblance of dignity. With not much hope in sight. They have no control over their lands, their security, their movement, their communication, their water supply. So when accords are signed and words like 'autonomy' and even 'statehood' are bandied about, it's always worth asking: What sort of autonomy? What sort of state? What sort of rights will its citizens have?

Young Palestinians who cannot contain their anger turn themselves into human bombs and haunt Israel's streets and public places, blowing themselves up, killing ordinary people, injecting terror into daily life, and eventually hardening both societies' suspicion and mutual hatred of each other. Each bombing invites merciless reprisals and even more hardship on Palestinian people. But then suicide bombing is an act of individual despair, not a revolutionary tactic. Although Palestinian attacks strike terror into Israeli civilians, they provide the perfect cover for the Israeli government's daily incursions into Palestinian territory, the perfect excuse for old-fashioned, nineteenth-century colonialism, dressed up as a new-fashioned, twenty-first-century war.

Israel's staunchest political and military ally is and always has been the US government. The US government has blocked, along with Israel, almost every UN resolution that sought a peaceful, equitable solution to the conflict.[23] It has supported almost every war that Israel has fought. When Israel attacks Palestine, it is American missiles that smash through Palestinian homes. And every year Israel receives several billion dollars from the United States. In addition to more than $3 billion annually in official Foreign Military

Financing, the US government supplies Israel with
economic assistance, loans, technology transfers, and
arms sales.[24]

What lessons should we draw from this tragic conflict? Is it really impossible for Jewish people who
suffered so cruelly themselves – more cruelly perhaps than any other people in history – to understand the vulnerability and the yearning of those
whom they have displaced? Does extreme suffering
always kindle cruelty? What hope does this leave the
human race with? What will happen to the Palestinian people in the event of a victory? When a nation
without a state eventually proclaims a state, what
kind of state will it be? What horrors will be per-
petrated under its flag? Is it a separate state that we
should be fighting for, or the rights to a life of liberty
and dignity for everyone regardless of their ethnicity
or religion?

Palestine was once a secular bulwark in the Middle
East. But now the weak, undemocratic, by all
accounts corrupt, but avowedly non-sectarian Palestinian Liberation Organization (PLO) is losing ground
to Hamas, which espouses an overtly sectarian ideology and fights in the name of Islam. To quote from
its manifesto: 'We will be its soldiers and the firewood
of its fire, which will burn the enemies.'[25]

The world is called upon to condemn suicide bombers. But can we ignore the long road they have journeyed on before they arrived at this destination? September 11th, 1922, to September 11th, 2002 – eighty years is a long, long time to have been waging war. Is there some advice the world can give the people of Palestine? Some scrap of hope we can hold out? Should they just settle for the crumbs that are thrown their way and behave like the grasshoppers or two-legged beasts they've been described as? Should they just take Golda Meir's suggestion and make a real effort to not exist?

In another part of the Middle East, September 11th strikes a more recent chord. It was on the 11th of September 1990 that George W. Bush Sr., then President of the United States, made a speech to a joint session of Congress announcing his government's decision to go to war against Iraq.[26]

The US government says that Saddam Hussein is a war criminal, a cruel military despot who has committed genocide against his own people. That's a fairly accurate description of the man. In 1988 he razed hundreds of villages in northern Iraq and used chemical weapons and machine-guns to kill thousands of Kurdish people. Today we know that that same year the US government provided him with five hundred million dollars in subsidies to buy American agricultural products. The next year, after he had successfully completed his genocidal campaign, the US government doubled its subsidy to one billion dollars.[27] It also provided him with high-quality germ seed for anthrax, as well as helicopters and dual-use material that could be used to manufacture chemical and biological weapons.[28]

So it turns out that while Saddam Hussein was carrying out his worst atrocities, the US and the UK governments were his close allies. Even today, the government of Turkey, which has one of the most appalling human-rights records in the world, is one of the US government's closest allies. The fact that the Turkish government has oppressed and murdered Kurdish people for years has not prevented the US government from plying Turkey with weapons and development aid.[29] Clearly it was not concern for the Kurdish people that provoked President Bush's speech to Congress.

What changed? In August 1990, Saddam Hussein invaded Kuwait. His sin was not so much that he had committed an act of war, but that he acted independently, without orders from his masters. This display of independence was enough to upset the power equation in the Gulf. So it was decided that Saddam Hussein be exterminated, like a pet that has outlived its owner's affection.

The first Allied attack on Iraq took place in January 1991. The world watched the prime-time war as it was played out on TV. (In India, those days, you had to go to a five-star hotel lobby to watch CNN.) Tens of thousands of people were killed in a month of devastating bombing.[30] What many do not know is that war did not end then. The initial fury simmered down into the longest sustained air attack on a country since the Vietnam War. Over the last decade, American and British forces have fired thousands of missiles and bombs on Iraq. Iraq's fields and farmlands have been shelled with three hundred tons of depleted uranium.[31] In their bombing sorties, the Allies targeted and destroyed water-treatment plants, aware of the fact that they could not be repaired without foreign assistance.[32] In southern Iraq, there has been a fourfold increase in cancer among children. In the decade of economic sanctions that followed the war, Iraqi civilians have been denied food, medicine, hospital equipment, ambulances, clean water – the basic essentials.[33]

About half a million Iraqi children have died as a result of the sanctions. Of them, Madeleine Albright, then US Ambassador to the United Nations, famously said, 'I think this is a very hard choice, but the price – we think the price is worth it.'[34] 'Moral equivalence' was the term that was used to denounce those who criticized the war on Afghanistan. Madeleine Albright cannot be accused of moral equivalence. What she said was just straightforward algebra.

A decade of bombing has not managed to dislodge Saddam Hussein, the 'Beast of Baghdad'. Now, almost twelve years on, President George Bush Jr. has ratcheted up the rhetoric once again. He's proposing an all-out war whose goal is nothing short of a 'regime change.' The *New York Times* says that the Bush administration is 'following a meticulously planned strategy to persuade the public, the Congress and the allies of the need to confront the threat of Saddam Hussein'. Andrew Card, the White House Chief of Staff, described how the administration was stepping up its war plans for the fall: 'From a marketing point of view,' he said, 'you don't introduce new products in August.'[35] This time the catchphrase for Washington's 'new product' is not the plight of the Kuwaiti people but the assertion that Iraq has weapons of mass destruction. Forget 'the feckless moralising of "peace" lobbies', wrote Richard Perle, chairman of the Defense Policy Board, the United States will 'act alone if necessary' and use a 'pre-emptive strike' if it determines it's in US interests.[36]

Weapons inspectors have conflicting reports about the status of Iraq's 'weapons of mass destruction', and many have said clearly that its arsenal has been dismantled and that it does not have the capacity to build one.[37] However, there is no confusion over the extent and range of America's arsenal of nuclear and chemical weapons. Would the US government welcome weapons inspectors? Would the UK? Or Israel? What if Iraq *does* have a nuclear weapon, does that justify a preemptive US strike? The United States has the largest arsenal of nuclear weapons in the world. It's the only country in the world to have actually used them on civilian populations. If the United States is justified in launching a preemptive attack on Iraq, why then any nuclear power is justified in carrying out a preemptive attack on any other. India could attack Pakistan, or the other way around. If the US government develops a distaste for the Indian Prime Minister, can it just 'take him out' with a preemptive strike? Recently the United States played an important part in forcing India and Pakistan back from the brink of war. Is it so hard for it to take its own advice? Who is guilty of feckless moralizing? Of preaching peace while it wages war? The United States, which George Bush calls 'a peaceful nation', has been at war with one country or another every year for the last fifty years.[38]

Wars are never fought for altruistic reasons. They're usually fought for hegemony, for business. And then, of course, there's the business of war. Protecting its control of the world's oil is fundamental to US foreign policy. The US government's recent military interventions in the Balkans and Central Asia have to do with oil. Hamid Karzai, the puppet president of Afghanistan installed by the United States, is said to be a former employee of Unocal, the American-based oil company.[39] The US government's paranoid patrolling of the Middle East is because it has two-thirds of the world's oil reserves.[40] Oil keeps America's engines purring sweetly. Oil keeps the free market rolling. Whoever controls the world's oil controls the world's markets.

And how do you control the oil? Nobody puts it more elegantly than the *New York Times* columnist Thomas Friedman. In an article called 'Craziness Pays', he says, 'the U.S. has to make clear to Iraq and US allies that . . . America will use force, without negotiation, hesitation, or UN approval'.[41] His advice was well taken. In the wars against Iraq and Afghanistan, as well as in the almost daily humiliation the US government heaps on the UN. In his book on globalization, *The Lexus and the Olive Tree*, Friedman says, 'The hidden hand of the market will never work without a hidden fist. McDonald's cannot flourish without McDonnell Douglas . . . And the hidden fist that keeps the world safe for Silicon Valley's technologies to flourish is called the US Army, Air Force, Navy, and Marine Corps.'[42]

Perhaps this was written in a moment of vulnerability, but it's certainly the most succinct, accurate description of the project of corporate globalization that I have read. After September 11th, 2001, and the War Against Terror, the hidden hand and fist have had their cover blown, and we have a clear view now of America's other weapon – the free market – bearing down on the developing world, with a clenched unsmiling smile. The Task That Does Not End is America's perfect war, the perfect vehicle for the endless expansion of American imperialism. In Urdu, the word for profit is *fayda*. *Al Qaeda* means The Word, The Word of God, The Law. So, in India some of us call the War Against Terror '*Al Qaeda* versus *Al Fayda*' – The Word versus The Profit (no pun intended). For the moment it looks as though *Al Fayda* will carry the day. But then you never know . . .

■

In the last ten years of unbridled corporate globalization, the world's total income has increased by an average of 2.5 per cent a year. And yet the number of the poor in the world has increased by one hundred million. Of the top hundred biggest economies, fifty-one are corporations, not countries. The top 1 per cent of the world has the same combined income as the bottom 57 per cent and the disparity is growing.[43] Now, under the spreading canopy of the War Against Terror, this process is being hustled along. The men in suits are in an unseemly hurry. While bombs rain down on us, and cruise missiles skid across the skies, while nuclear weapons are stockpiled to make the world a safer place, contracts are being signed, patents are being registered, oil pipelines are being laid, natural resources are being plundered, water is being privatized, and democracies are being undermined.

In a country like India, the 'structural adjustment' end of the corporate globalization project is ripping through people's lives. 'Development' projects, massive privatization, and labour 'reforms' are pushing people off their lands and out of their jobs, resulting in a kind of barbaric dispossession that has few parallels in history. Across the world, as the free market brazenly protects western markets and forces developing countries to lift their trade barriers, the poor are getting poorer and the rich richer. Civil unrest has begun to erupt in the global village. In countries like Argentina, Brazil, Mexico, Bolivia, and India, the resistance movements against corporate globalization are growing. To contain them, governments are tightening their control. Protesters are being labelled 'terrorists' and then being dealt with as such. But civil unrest does not only mean marches and demonstrations and protests against globalization. Unfortunately, it also means a desperate downward spiral into crime and chaos and all kinds of despair and disillusionment which, as we know from history (and from what we see un-spooling before our eyes), gradually becomes a fertile breeding ground for terrible things – cultural nationalism, religious bigotry, fascism, and of course terrorism.

All these march arm in arm with corporate globalization.

There is a notion gaining credence that the free market breaks down national barriers, and that corporate globalization's ultimate destination is a hippie paradise where the heart is the only passport and we all live together happily inside a John Lennon song (*Imagine there's no countries . . .*). This is a canard.

What the free market undermines is not national sovereignty, but *democracy*. As the disparity between the rich and poor grows, the hidden fist has its work cut out for it. Multinational corporations on the prowl for sweetheart deals that yield enormous profits cannot push through those deals and administer those projects in developing countries without the active connivance of state machinery – the police, the courts, sometimes even the army. Today corporate globalization needs an international confederation of loyal, corrupt, authoritarian governments in poorer countries to push through unpopular reforms and quell the mutinies. It needs a press that pretends to be free. It needs courts that pretend to dispense justice. It needs nuclear bombs, standing armies, sterner immigration laws, and watchful coastal patrols to make sure that it's only money, goods, patents, and services that are globalized – not the free movement of people, not a respect for human rights, not international treaties on racial discrimination, or chemical and nuclear weapons, or greenhouse gas emissions, climate change, or, God forbid, justice.[44] It's as though even a *gesture* towards international accountability would wreck the whole enterprise.

Close to one year after the War Against Terror was officially flagged off in the ruins of Afghanistan, freedoms are being curtailed in country after country in the name of protecting freedom, civil liberties are being suspended in the name of protecting democracy.[45] All kinds of dissent is being defined as 'terrorism'. All kinds of laws are being passed to deal with it. Osama bin Laden seems to have vanished into thin air. Mullah Omar is said to have made his escape on a motorbike.[46] (They could have sent Tintin after him.) The Taliban may have disappeared but their spirit, and their system of summary justice, is surfacing in the unlikeliest of places. In India, in Pakistan, in Nigeria, in America, in all the Central Asian republics run by all manner of despots, and of course in Afghanistan under the US-backed Northern Alliance.[47]

■

Meanwhile, down at the mall there's a mid-season sale. Everything's discounted – oceans, rivers, oil, gene pools, fig wasps, flowers, childhoods, aluminum factories, phone companies, wisdom, wilderness, civil rights, ecosystems, air – all 4.6 billion years of evolution. It's packed, sealed, tagged, valued, and available off the rack (no returns). As for justice – I'm told it's on offer too. You can get the best that money can buy.

Donald Rumsfeld said that his mission in the War Against Terror was to persuade the world that Americans must be allowed to continue their way of life.[48] When the maddened king stamps his foot, slaves tremble in their quarters. So, standing here today, it's hard for me to say this, but The American Way of Life is simply not sustainable. Because it doesn't acknowledge that there is a world beyond America.

Fortunately, power has a shelf life. When the time comes, maybe this mighty empire will, like others before it, overreach itself and implode from within. It looks as though structural cracks have already appeared. As the War Against Terror casts its net wider and wider, America's corporate heart is haemorrhaging. For all the endless empty chatter about democracy, today the world is run by three of the most secretive institutions in the world: the International Monetary Fund, the World Bank, and the World Trade Organization, all three of which, in turn, are dominated by the United States. Their decisions are made in secret. The people who head them are appointed behind closed doors. Nobody really knows anything about them, their politics, their beliefs, their intentions. Nobody elected them. Nobody said they could make decisions on our behalf. A world run by a handful of greedy bankers and CEOs who nobody elected can't possibly last.

Soviet-style Communism failed, not because it was intrinsically evil, but because it was flawed. It allowed too few people to usurp too much power. Twenty-first-century market capitalism, American-style, will fail for the same reasons. Both are edifices constructed by human intelligence, undone by human nature.

The time has come, the Walrus said. Perhaps things will get worse and then better. Perhaps there's a small god up in heaven readying herself for us. Another world is not only possible, she's on her way. Maybe many of us won't be here to greet her, but on a quiet day, if I listen very carefully, I can hear her breathing.

the loneliness of noam chomsky

the loneliness of noam chomsky

'I will never apologize for the United States of America – I don't care what the facts are.' – President George Bush Sr.[1]

Sitting in my home in New Delhi, watching an American TV news channel promote itself ('We report. You decide'), I imagine Noam Chomsky's amused, chipped-tooth smile.

Everybody knows that authoritarian regimes, regardless of their ideology, use the mass media for propaganda. But what about democratically elected regimes in the 'free world'?

Today, thanks to Noam Chomsky and his fellow media analysts, it is almost axiomatic for thousands, possibly millions, of us that public opinion in 'free market' democracies is manufactured just like any other mass-market product – soap, switches, or sliced bread.[2] We know that while, legally and constitutionally, speech may be free, the space in which that freedom can be exercised has been snatched from us and auctioned to the highest bidders. Neo-liberal capitalism isn't just about the accumulation of capital (for some). It's also about the accumulation of power (for some), the accumulation of freedom (for some). Conversely, for the rest of the world, the people who are excluded from neo-liberalism's governing body, it's about the *erosion* of capital, the *erosion* of power, the *erosion* of freedom. In the 'free' market, free speech has become a commodity like everything else – justice, human rights, drinking water, clean air. It's available only to those who can afford it. And naturally, those who can afford it use free speech to manufacture the kind of product, confect the kind of public opinion, that best suits their purpose. (News they can use.) Exactly how they do this has been the subject of much of Noam Chomsky's political writing.

Prime Minister Silvio Berlusconi, for instance, has a controlling interest in major Italian newspapers, magazines, television channels, and publishing houses. '[T]he prime minister in effect controls about 90 per cent of Italian TV viewership,' reports the *Financial Times*.[3]

What price free speech? Free speech for *whom*? Admittedly, Berlusconi is an extreme example. In other democracies – the United States in particular –

media barons, powerful corporate lobbies, and government officials are imbricated in a more elaborate but less obvious manner. (George Bush Jr.'s connections to the oil lobby, to the arms industry, and to Enron, and Enron's infiltration of U.S. government institutions and the mass media – all this is public knowledge now.)

After the September 11th terrorist strikes in New York and Washington, the mainstream media's blatant performance as the US government's mouthpiece, its display of vengeful patriotism, its willingness to publish Pentagon press handouts as news, and its explicit censorship of dissenting opinion became the butt of some pretty black humour in the rest of the world.

Then the New York Stock Exchange crashed, bankrupt airline companies appealed to the government for financial bailouts, and there was talk of circumventing patent laws in order to manufacture generic drugs to fight the anthrax scare (*much* more important and urgent of course than the production of generics to fight AIDS in Africa).[4]

Suddenly, it began to seem as though the twin myths of Free Speech and the Free Market might come crashing down alongside the Twin Towers of the World Trade Center.

But of course that never happened. The myths live on.

There is however, a brighter side to the amount of energy and money that the establishment pours into the business of 'managing' public opinion. It suggests a very real *fear* of public opinion. It suggests a persistent and valid worry that if people were to discover (and fully comprehend) the real nature of the things that are done in their name, they might *act* upon that knowledge. Powerful people know that ordinary people are not always reflexively ruthless and selfish. (When ordinary people weigh costs and benefits, something like an uneasy conscience could easily tip the scales.) For this reason, they must be guarded against reality, reared in a controlled climate, in an altered reality, like broiler chickens or pigs in a pen.

Those of us who have managed to escape this fate and are scratching about in the backyard no longer believe everything we read in the papers and watch on TV. We put our ears to the ground and look for other ways of making sense of the world. We search for the untold story, the mentioned-in-passing military coup, the unreported genocide, the civil war in an African country written up in a one-column-inch story next to a full-page advertisement for lace underwear.

We don't always remember, and many don't even know, that this way of thinking, this easy acuity, this instinctive mistrust of the mass media, would at best be a political hunch and at worst a loose accusation if it were not for the relentless and unswerving media analysis of one of the world's greatest minds. And this is only *one* of the ways in which Noam Chomsky has radically altered our understanding of the society in which we live. Or should I say, our understanding of the elaborate rules of the lunatic asylum in which we are all voluntary inmates?

Speaking about the September 11th attacks in New York and Washington, President George W. Bush called the enemies of the United States 'enemies of freedom'. 'Americans are asking why do they hate us?' he said. 'They hate our freedoms, our freedom of religion, our freedom of speech, our freedom to vote and assemble and disagree with each other.'⁵

If people in the United States want a real answer to that question (as opposed to the ones in the *Idiot's Guide to Anti-Americanism*, that is: 'Because they're jealous of us', 'Because they hate freedom', 'Because they're losers', 'Because we're good and they're evil'), I'd say, read Chomsky. Read Chomsky on US military interventions in Indochina, Latin America, Iraq, Bosnia, the former Yugoslavia,

Afghanistan and the Middle East. If ordinary people in the United States read Chomsky, perhaps their questions would be framed a little differently. Perhaps it would be: 'Why don't they hate us more than they do?' or 'Isn't it surprising that September 11th didn't happen earlier?'

Unfortunately, in these nationalistic times, words like 'us' and 'them' are used loosely. The line between citizens and the state is being deliberately and successfully blurred, not just by governments, but also by terrorists. The underlying logic of terrorist attacks, as well as 'retaliatory' wars against governments that 'support terrorism', is the same: both punish citizens for the actions of their governments.

If I were asked to choose *one* of Noam Chomsky's major contributions to the world, it would be the fact that he has unmasked the ugly, manipulative, ruthless universe that exists behind that beautiful, sunny word 'freedom'. He has done this rationally and empirically. The mass of evidence he has marshalled to construct his case is formidable. Terrifying, actually. The starting premise of Chomsky's method is not ideological, but it *is* intensely political. He embarks on his course of inquiry with an anarchist's instinctive mistrust of power. He takes us on a tour through the bog of the US establishment, and leads us through the dizzying maze of corridors that connects the government, big business, and the business of managing public opinion.

Chomsky shows us how phrases like 'free speech', the 'free market', and the 'free world' have little, if anything, to do with freedom. He shows us that, among the myriad freedoms claimed by the US government are the freedom to murder, annihilate, and dominate other people. The freedom to finance and sponsor despots and dictators across the world. The freedom to train, arm, and shelter terrorists. The freedom to topple democratically elected governments. The freedom to amass and use weapons of mass destruction – chemical, biological, and nuclear. The freedom to go to war against any country whose government it disagrees with. And, most terrible of all, the freedom to commit these crimes against humanity in the name of 'justice', in the name of 'righteousness', in the name of 'freedom'.

Attorney General John Ashcroft has declared that US freedoms are 'not the grant of any government or document, but . . . our endowment from God'.[6] So, basically, we're confronted with a country armed with a mandate from heaven. Perhaps this explains why the US government refuses to judge itself by the same moral standards by which it judges others. (Any attempt to do this is shouted down as 'moral equivalence'.) Its technique is to position itself as the

well-intentioned giant whose good deeds are con-
founded in strange countries by their scheming
natives, whose markets it's trying to free, whose societies it's trying to modernize, whose women it's trying
to liberate, whose souls it's trying to save.

Perhaps this belief in its own divinity also explains
why the US government has conferred upon itself the
right and freedom to murder and exterminate people
'for their own good'.

When he announced the US air strikes against
Afghanistan, President Bush Jr. said, 'We're a peaceful
nation.'[7] He went on to say, 'This is the calling of the
United States of America, the most free nation in the
world, a nation built on fundamental values, that
rejects hate, rejects violence, rejects murderers, rejects
evil. And we will not tire.'[8]

The US empire rests on a grisly foundation: the massacre of millions of indigenous people, the stealing of
their lands and, following this, the kidnapping and
enslavement of millions of black people from Africa
to work that land. Thousands died on the seas while
they were being shipped like caged cattle between
continents.[9]

'Stolen from Africa, brought to America' – Bob Marley's 'Buffalo Soldier' contains a whole universe of unspeakable sadness.[10] It tells of the loss of dignity, the loss of wilderness, the loss of freedom, the shattered pride of a people. Genocide and slavery provide the social and economic underpinning of the nation whose fundamental values reject hate, murderers, and evil.

Here is Chomsky, writing in the essay 'The Manufacture of Consent', on the founding of the United States of America:

> *During the Thanksgiving holiday a few weeks ago, I took a walk with some friends and family in a national park. We came across a gravestone, which had on it the following inscription: 'Here lies an Indian woman, a Wampanoag, whose family and tribe gave of themselves and their land that this great nation might be born and grow.'*

> *Of course, it is not quite accurate to say that the indigenous population gave of themselves and their land for that noble purpose. Rather, they were slaughtered, decimated, and dispersed in the course of one of the greatest exercises in genocide in human history . . . which we celebrate each October when we honor Columbus – a notable mass murderer himself – on Columbus Day.*

> *Hundreds of American citizens, well-meaning and decent people, troop by that gravestone regularly and read it, apparently without reaction; except, perhaps, a feeling of satisfaction that at last we are giving some due recognition to the sacrifices of the native peoples ... They might react differently if they were to visit Auschwitz or Dachau and find a gravestone reading: 'Here lies a woman, a Jew, whose family and people gave of themselves and their possessions that this great nation might grow and prosper.'[11]*

How has the United States survived its terrible past and emerged smelling so sweet? Not by owning up to it, not by making reparations, not by apologizing to black Americans or native Americans, and certainly not by changing its ways (it *exports* its cruelties now). Like most other countries, the United States has rewritten its history. But what sets the United States apart from other countries, and puts it way ahead in the race, is that it has enlisted the services of the most powerful, most successful publicity firm in the world: Hollywood.

In the best-selling version of popular myth as history, US 'goodness' peaked during World War II (a.k.a. America's War Against Fascism). Lost in the din of trumpet sound and angel song is the fact that when fascism was in full stride in Europe, the US government actually looked away. When Hitler was carrying out his genocidal pogrom against Jews, US officials refused entry to Jewish refugees fleeing Germany. The United States entered the war only *after* the Japanese bombed Pearl Harbor. Drowned out by the noisy hosannas is its most barbaric act, in fact the single most savage act the world has ever witnessed: the dropping of the atomic bomb on civilian populations in Hiroshima and Nagasaki. The war was nearly over. The hundreds of thousands of Japanese people who were killed, the countless others who were crippled by cancers for generations to come, were not a threat to world peace. They were *civilians*. Just as the victims of the World Trade Center and Pentagon bombings were civilians. Just as the hundreds of thousands of people who died in Iraq because of the US-led sanctions were civilians. The bombing of Hiroshima and Nagasaki was a cold, calculated experiment carried out to demonstrate America's power. At the time, President Truman described it as 'the greatest thing in history'.[12]

The Second World War, we're told, was a 'war for peace'. The atomic bomb was a 'weapon of peace'. We're invited to believe that nuclear deterrence prevented World War III. (That was before President George Bush Jr. came up with the 'pre-emptive strike doctrine'.)[13] *Was* there an outbreak of peace after the Second World War? Certainly there was (relative) peace in Europe and America – but does that count as world peace? Not unless savage, proxy wars fought in lands where the coloured races live (chinks, niggers, dinks, wogs, gooks) don't count as wars at all.

Since the Second World War, the United States has been at war with or has attacked, among other countries, Korea, Guatemala, Cuba, Laos, Vietnam, Cambodia, Grenada, Libya, El Salvador, Nicaragua, Panama, Iraq, Somalia, Sudan, Yugoslavia, and Afghanistan. This list should also include the US government's covert operations in Africa, Asia, and Latin America, the coups it has engineered, and the dictators it has armed and supported. It should include Israel's US-backed war on Lebanon, in which thousands were killed. It should include the key role America has played in the conflict in the Middle East, in which thousands have died fighting Israel's illegal occupation of Palestinian territory. It should include America's role in the civil war in Afghanistan in the 1980s, in which more than one million people were killed.[14] It should include the embargoes and sanctions that have led directly and indirectly to the death of hundreds of thousands of people, most visibly in Iraq.[15] Put it all together, and it sounds very much as though there has been a World War III, and that the US government was (or is) one of its chief protagonists.

Most of the essays in Chomsky's *For Reasons of State* are about US aggression in South Vietnam, North Vietnam, Laos, and Cambodia. It was a war that lasted more than twelve years. Fifty-eight thousand Americans and approximately two million Vietnamese, Cambodians, and Laotians lost their lives.[16] The US deployed half a million ground troops, dropped more than six million tons of bombs.[17] And yet, though you wouldn't believe it if you watched most Hollywood movies, America lost the war.

The war began in South Vietnam and then spread to North Vietnam, Laos, and Cambodia. After putting in place a client regime in Saigon, the US government invited itself in to fight a Communist insurgency – Vietcong guerrillas who had infiltrated rural regions of South Vietnam where villagers were sheltering them. This was exactly the model that Russia replicated when, in 1979, it invited itself into Afghanistan. Nobody in the 'free world' is in any doubt about the fact that Russia invaded Afghanistan. After *glasnost*, even a Soviet foreign minister called the Soviet invasion of Afghanistan 'illegal and immoral'.[18] But there has been no such introspection in the United States. In 1984, in a stunning revelation, Chomsky wrote:

> *For the past twenty-two years, I have been search-*
> *ing to find some reference in mainstream journal-*

> *ism or scholarship to an American invasion of*
> *South Vietnam in 1962 (or ever), or an American*
> *attack against South Vietnam, or American aggres-*
> *sion in Indochina – without success. There is no*
> *such event in history. Rather, there is an American*
> defense *of South Vietnam against terrorists sup-*
> *ported from the outside (namely from Vietnam).*[19]

There is no such event in history!

In 1962, the US Air Force began to bomb rural South
Vietnam, where 80 per cent of the population lived.
The bombing lasted for more than a decade. Thousands of people were killed. The idea was to bomb on a
scale colossal enough to induce panic migration from
villages into cities, were people could be held in refugee camps. Samuel Huntington referred to this as a
process of 'urbanization'.[20] (I learned about urbanization when I was in architecture school in India.
Somehow I don't remember aerial bombing being part
of the syllabus.) Huntington – famous today for his
essay 'The Clash of Civilizations?' – was at the time
Chairman of the Council on Vietnamese Studies of
the Southeast Asia Development Advisory Group.
Chomsky quotes him describing the Vietcong as 'a
powerful force which cannot be dislodged from its
constituency so long as the constituency continues to
exist'.[21] Huntington went on to advise 'direct applica-
tion of mechanical and conventional power' – in other

words, to crush a people's war, eliminate the people.[22] (Or, perhaps, to update the thesis – in order to prevent a clash of civilizations, annihilate a civilization.)

Here's one observer from the time on the limitations of America's mechanical power: 'The problem is that American machines are not equal to the task of killing communist soldiers except as part of a scorched-earth policy that destroys everything else as well.'[23] That problem has been solved now. Not with less destructive bombs, but with more imaginative language. There's a more elegant way of saying 'that destroys everything else as well'. The phrase is 'collateral damage'. And here's a first-hand account of what America's 'machines' (Huntington called them 'modernizing instruments' and staff officers in the Pentagon called them 'bomb-o-grams') can do.[24] This is T. D. Allman flying over the Plain of Jars in Laos.

> Even if the war in Laos ended tomorrow, the restoration of its ecological balance might take several years. The reconstruction of the Plain's totally destroyed towns and villages might take just as long. Even if this was done, the Plain might long prove perilous to human habitation because of the hundreds of thousands of unexploded bombs, mines and booby traps.

A recent flight around the Plain of Jars revealed what less than three years of intensive American bombing can do to a rural area, even after its civilian population has been evacuated. In large areas, the primary tropical colour – bright green – has been replaced by an abstract pattern of black, and bright metallic colours. Much of the remaining foliage is stunted, dulled by defoliants.

Today, black is the dominant colour of the northern and eastern reaches of the Plain. Napalm is dropped regularly to burn off the grass and undergrowth that covers the Plains and fills its many narrow ravines. The fires seem to burn constantly, creating rectangles of black. During the flight, plumes of smoke could be seen rising from freshly bombed areas.

The main routes, coming into the Plain from communist-held territory, are bombed mercilessly, apparently on a non-stop basis. There, and along the rim of the Plain, the dominant colour is yellow. All vegetation has been destroyed. The craters are countless ... [T]he area has been bombed so repeatedly that the land resembles the pocked, churned desert in storm-hit areas of the North African desert.

Further to the southeast, Xieng Khouangville – once the most populous town in communist Laos –

lies empty, destroyed. To the north of the Plain, the little resort of Khang Khay also has been destroyed.

Around the landing field at the base of King Kong, the main colours are yellow (from upturned soil) and black (from napalm), relieved by patches of bright red and blue: parachutes used to drop supplies.

[T]he last local inhabitants were being carted into air transports. Abandoned vegetable gardens that would never be harvested grew near abandoned houses with plates still on the tables and calendars on the walls.[25]

(Never counted in the 'costs' of war are the dead birds, the charred animals, the murdered fish, incinerated insects, poisoned water sources, destroyed vegetation. Rarely mentioned is the arrogance of the human race towards other living things with which it shares this planet. All these are forgotten in the fight for markets and ideologies. This arrogance will probably be the ultimate undoing of the human species.)

The centrepiece of *For Reasons of State* is an essay called 'The Mentality of the Backroom Boys', in which Chomsky offers an extraordinarily supple, exhaustive analysis of the Pentagon Papers, which he says 'provide documentary evidence of a conspiracy to use force in international affairs in violation of law'.[26] Here, too, Chomsky makes note of the fact that while the bombing of North Vietnam is discussed at some length in the Pentagon Papers, the invasion of South Vietnam barely merits a mention.[27]

The Pentagon Papers are mesmerizing, not as documentation of the history of the US war in Indochina, but as insight into the minds of the men who planned and executed it. It's fascinating to be privy to the ideas that were being tossed around, the suggestions that were made, the proposals that were put forward. In a section called 'The Asian Mind – the American Mind', Chomsky examines the discussion of the mentality of the enemy that 'stoically accept[s] the destruction of wealth and the loss of lives', whereas 'We want life, happiness, wealth, power', and, for us, 'death and suffering are irrational choices when alternatives exist'.[28] So, we learn that the Asian poor, presumably because they cannot comprehend the meaning of happiness, wealth, and power, invite America to carry this 'strategic logic to its conclusion, which is genocide'. But, then 'we' balk because 'genocide is a terrible burden to bear'.[29] (Eventually, of course, 'we' went ahead and committed genocide anyway, and then pretended that it never really happened.)

Of course, the Pentagon Papers contain some moderate proposals, as well: 'Destruction of locks and dams, however – if handled right – might . . . offer promise. It should be studied. Such destruction does not kill or drown people. By shallow-flooding the rice, it leads after time to widespread starvation (more than a million?) unless food is provided – which we could offer to do 'at the conference table'.'[30]

Layer by layer, Chomsky strips down the process of decision-making by US government officials, to reveal at its core the pitiless heart of the American war machine, completely insulated from the realities of war, blinded by ideology, and willing to annihilate millions of human beings, civilians, soldiers, women, children, villages, whole cities, whole ecosystems – with scientifically honed methods of brutality. Here's an American pilot talking about the joys of napalm:

> We sure are pleased with those backroom boys at Dow. The original product wasn't so hot – if the gooks were quick they could scrape it off. So the boys started adding polystyrene – now it sticks like shit to a blanket. But then if the gooks jumped under water it stopped burning, so they started adding Willie Peter [white phosphorous] so's to make it burn better. It'll even burn under water now. And just one drop is enough, it'll keep on

burning right down to the bone so they die anyway
from phosphorus poisoning.[31]

So the lucky gooks were annihilated for their own
good. Better Dead than Red. Thanks to the seductive
charms of Hollywood and the irresistible appeal of
America's mass media, all these years later, the world
views the war as an *American* story. Indochina provided the lush, tropical backdrop against which the
United States played out its fantasies of violence,
tested its latest technology, furthered its ideology,
examined its conscience, agonized over its moral
dilemmas, and dealt with its guilt (or pretended
to). The Vietnamese, the Cambodians, and Laotians
were only script props. Nameless, faceless, slit-eyed
humanoids. They were just the people who died.
Gooks.

The only real lesson the US government learned from
its invasion of Indochina is how to go to war without
committing American troops and risking American
lives. So now we have wars waged with long-range
cruise missiles, Black Hawks, 'bunker busters'. Wars
in which the 'Allies' lose more journalists than soldiers. As a child growing up in the state of Kerala, in
South India – where the first democratically elected
Communist government in the world came to power
in 1959, the year I was born – I worried terribly about
being a gook. Kerala was only a few thousand miles

west of Vietnam. We had jungles and rivers and rice-fields, and Communists, too. I kept imagining my mother, my brother, and myself being blown out of the bushes by a grenade, or mowed down, like the gooks in the movies, by an American marine with muscled arms and chewing gum and a loud background score. In my dreams, I was the burning girl in the famous photograph taken on the road from Trang Bang. As someone who grew up on the cusp of both American and Soviet propaganda (which more or less neutralized each other), when I first read Noam Chomsky, it occurred to me that his marshalling of evidence, the volume of it, the relentlessness of it, was a little – how shall I put it? – insane. Even a quarter of the evidence he had compiled would have been enough to convince me. I used to wonder why he needed to do so much *work*. But now I understand that the magnitude and intensity of Chomsky's work is a barometer of the magnitude, scope, and relentlessness of the propaganda machine that he's up against. He's like the wood-borer who lives inside the third rack of my bookshelf. Day and night, I hear his jaws crunching through the wood, grinding it to a fine dust. It's as though he disagrees with the literature and wants to destroy the very structure on which it rests. I call him Chompsky.

Being an American working in America, writing to convince Americans of his point of view must really be like having to tunnel through hard wood. Chomsky is one of a small band of individuals fighting a whole industry. And that makes him not only brilliant, but heroic.

Some years ago, in a poignant interview with James Peck, Chomsky spoke about his memory of the day Hiroshima was bombed. He was sixteen years old:

> *I remember that I literally couldn't talk to any-body. There was nobody. I just walked off by myself. I was at a summer camp at the time, and I walked off into the woods and stayed alone for a couple of hours when I heard about it. I could never talk to anyone about it and never understood anyone's reaction. I felt completely isolated.*[32]

That isolation produced one of the greatest, most radical public thinkers of our time. When the sun sets on the American empire, as it will, as it must, Noam Chomsky's work will survive. It will point a cool, incriminating finger at a merciless, Machiavellian empire as cruel, self-righteous, and hypocritical as the ones it has replaced. (The only difference is that it is armed with technology that can visit the kind of devastation on the world that history has never known and the human race cannot begin to imagine.) As a could've-been gook, and who knows, perhaps a potential gook, hardly a day goes by when I don't find myself thinking – for one reason or another – 'Chomsky Zindabad'.

confronting empire

confronting empire

I've been asked to speak about 'How to confront Empire?' It's as huge question, and I have no easy answers.

When we speak of confronting Empire, we need to identify what Empire means. Does it mean the US government (and its European satellites), the World Bank, the International Monetary Fund, the World Trade Organization (WTO), and multinational corporations? Or is it something more than that?

In many countries, Empire has sprouted other subsidiary heads, some dangerous by-products – nationalism, religious bigotry, fascism and, of course, terrorism. All these march arm in arm with the project of corporate globalization.

Let me illustrate what I mean. India – the world's biggest democracy – is currently at the forefront of the corporate globalization project. Its 'market' of one

billion people is being pried open by the WTO. Corporatization and privatization are being welcomed by
the government and the Indian elite.

It is not a coincidence that the Prime Minister,
the Home Minister, the Disinvestment Minister – the
men who signed the deal with Enron in India, the men
who are selling the country's infrastructure to corporate multinationals, the men who want to privatize
water, electricity, oil, coal, steel, health, education,
and telecommunication – are all members or admirers
of the Rashtriya Swayamsevak Sangh (RSS), a right-
wing, ultra-nationalist Hindu guild which has openly
admired Hitler and his methods.

The dismantling of democracy is proceeding with the
speed and efficiency of a Structural Adjustment Pro-
gram. While the project of corporate globalization rips
through people's lives in India, massive privatization
and labour 'reforms' are pushing people off their land
and out of their jobs. Hundreds of impoverished
farmers are committing suicide by consuming pesti-
cide.[1] Reports of starvation deaths are coming in from
all over the country.[2]

While the elite journeys to its imaginary destination
somewhere near the top of the world, the dispossessed
are spiralling downwards into crime and chaos. This
climate of frustration and national disillusionment is

the perfect breeding ground, history tells us, for fascism.

The two arms of the Indian government have evolved the perfect pincer action. While one arm is busy selling India off in chunks, the other, to divert attention, is orchestrating a howling, baying chorus of Hindu nationalism and religious fascism. It is conducting nuclear tests, rewriting history books, burning churches, and demolishing mosques. Censorship, surveillance, the suspension of civil liberties and human rights, the questioning of who is an Indian citizen and who is not, particularly with regard to religious minorities, are all becoming common practice now.

Last March, in the state of Gujarat, two thousand Muslims were butchered in a state-sponsored pogrom. Muslim women were specially targeted. They were stripped, and gang-raped, before being burned alive. Arsonists burned and looted shops, homes, textiles mills, and mosques.[3] More than a hundred and fifty thousand Muslims have been driven from their homes. The economic base of the Muslim community has been devastated. While Gujarat burned, the Indian Prime Minister was on MTV promoting his new poems. In December 2002, the government that orchestrated the killing was voted back into office with a comfortable majority.[4] Nobody has been punished for the genocide. Narendra Modi, architect of the pogrom, proud member of the RSS, has embarked on his second term as the Chief Minister of Gujarat. If he were Saddam Hussein, of course, each atrocity would have been on CNN. But since he's not – and since the Indian 'market' is open to global investors – the massacre is not even an embarrassing inconvenience. There are more than one hundred million Muslims in India. A time bomb is ticking in our ancient land.

All this is to say that it is a myth that the free market breaks down national barriers. The free market does not threaten national sovereignty, it undermines democracy. As the disparity between the rich and the poor grows, the fight to corner resources is intensifying. To push through their 'sweetheart deals', to corporatize the crops we grow, the water we drink, the air we breathe, and the dreams we dream, corporate globalization needs an international confederation of loyal, corrupt, authoritarian governments in poorer countries to push through unpopular reforms and quell the mutinies. Corporate globalization – or shall we call it by its name? Imperialism – needs a press that pretends to be free. It needs courts that pretend to dispense justice.

Meanwhile, the countries of the north harden their borders and stockpile weapons of mass destruction.

After all, they have to make sure that it's only money, goods, patents, and services that are globalized. Not the free movement of people. Not a respect for human rights. Not international treaties on racial discrimination or chemical and nuclear weapons or greenhouse gas emissions or climate change or – God forbid – justice.

So this – *all* this – is Empire. This loyal confederation, this obscene accumulation of power, this greatly increased distance between those who make the decisions and those who have to suffer them.

Our fight, our goal, our vision of another world must be to eliminate that distance. So how do we resist Empire?

The good news is that we're not doing too badly. There have been major victories. Here in Latin America you have had so many – in Bolivia, you have Cochabamba.[5] In Peru, there was the uprising in Arequipa.[6] In Venezuela, President Hugo Chavez is holding on, despite the US government's best efforts.[7] And the world's gaze is on the people of Argentina, who are trying to refashion a country from the ashes of the havoc wrought by the IMF.[8]

In India the movement against corporate globalization is gathering momentum and is poised to become the only real political force to counter religious fascism.

As for corporate globalization's glittering ambassadors – Enron, Bechtel, WorldCom, Arthur Andersen – where were they last year, and where are they now?

And of course here in Brazil we must ask: who was the president last year, and who is it now?

Still, many of us have dark moments of hopelessness and despair. We know that under the spreading canopy of the War Against Terrorism, the men in suits are hard at work. While bombs rain down on us and cruise missiles skid across the skies, we know that contracts are being signed, patents are being registered, oil pipelines are being laid, natural resources are being plundered, water is being privatized, and George Bush is planning to go to war against Iraq.

If we look at this conflict as a straightforward eyeball to eyeball confrontation between Empire and those of us who are resisting it, it might seem that we are losing.

But there is another way of looking at it. We, all of us gathered here, have, each in our own way, laid siege to Empire.

We may not have stopped it in its tracks – yet – but we have stripped it down. We have made it drop its mask. We have forced it into the open. It now stands before us on the world's stage in all its brutish, iniquitous nakedness. Empire may well go to war, but it's out in the open now – too ugly to behold its own reflection. Too ugly even to rally its own people. It won't be long before the majority of American people become our allies.

In Washington a quarter of a million people marched against the war on Iraq.[9] Each month, the protest is gathering momentum. Before September 11th, 2001, America had a secret history. Secret especially from its own people. But now America's secrets are history, and its history is public knowledge. It's street talk.

Today, we know that every argument that is being used to escalate the war against Iraq is a lie. The most ludicrous of them being the US government's deep commitment to bring democracy to Iraq. Killing people to save them from dictatorship or ideological corruption is, of course, an old US government sport. Here in Latin America, you know that better than most. Nobody doubts that Saddam Hussein is a ruthless dictator, a murderer (whose worst excesses were supported by the governments of the United States and Great Britain). There's no doubt that Iraqis would be better off without him.

But, then, the whole world would be better off without a certain Mr Bush. In fact, he is far more dangerous than Saddam Hussein.

So, should we bomb Bush out of the White House?

It's more than clear that Bush is determined to go to war against Iraq, *regardless* of the facts – and regardless of international public opinion. In its recruitment drive for allies, the United States is prepared to *invent* facts. The charade with weapons inspectors is the US government's offensive, insulting concession to some twisted form of international etiquette. It's like leaving the 'doggie door' open for last-minute 'allies' or maybe the United Nations to crawl through. But for all intents and purposes, the new war against Iraq has begun.

What can we do?

We can hone our memory, we can learn from our history. We can continue to build public opinion until it becomes a deafening roar.

We can turn the war on Iraq into a fishbowl of the US government's excesses.

We can expose George Bush and Tony Blair – and their allies – for the cowardly baby-killers, water poisoners, and pusillanimous long-distance bombers that they are. We can re-invent civil disobedience in a million different ways. In other words, we can come up with a million ways of becoming a collective pain in the ass.

When George Bush says 'You're either with us, or you are with the terrorists', we can say 'No thank you'. We can let him know that the people of the world do not need to choose between a Malevolent Mickey Mouse and the Mad Mullahs.

Our strategy should be not only to confront Empire, but to lay siege to it. To deprive it of oxygen. To shame it. To mock it. With our art, our music, our literature, our stubbornness, our joy, our brilliance, our sheer relentlessness – and our ability to tell our own stories. Stories that are different from the ones we're being brainwashed to believe. The corporate revolution will collapse if we refuse to buy what they are selling – their ideas, their version of history, their wars, their weapons, their notion of inevitability. Remember this: We be many and they be few. They need us more than we need them.

the ordinary person's guide
to empire

the ordinary person's guide to empire

Mesopotamia. Babylon. The Tigris and Euphrates. How many children in how many classrooms, over how many centuries, have hang-glided through the past, transported on the wings of these words?

And now the bombs are falling, incinerating and humiliating that ancient civilization.

On the steel torsos of their missiles, adolescent American soldiers scrawl colourful messages in childish handwriting: *For Saddam, from the Fat Boy Posse*. A building goes down. A market-place. A home. A girl who loves a boy. A child who only ever wanted to play with his older brother's marbles.

On 21 March, the day after American and British troops began their illegal invasion and occupation of Iraq, an 'embedded' CNN correspondent interviewed an American soldier. 'I wanna get in there and get my nose dirty,' Private AJ said. 'I wanna take revenge for 9/11.'

To be fair to the correspondent, even though he *was* 'embedded', he *did* sort of weakly suggest that so far there was no real evidence that linked the Iraqi government to the September 11th attacks. Private AJ stuck his teenage tongue out all the way down to the end of his chin. 'Yeah, well, that stuff's way over my head,' he said.

According to a *New York Times/CBS News* survey, 42 per cent of the American public believes that Saddam Hussein is directly responsible for the September 11th attacks on the World Trade Center and the Pentagon. And an ABC news poll says that 55 per cent of Americans believe that Saddam Hussein directly supports Al Qaeda. What percentage of America's armed forces believes these fabrications is anybody's guess.

■

It is unlikely that British and American troops fighting in Iraq are aware that their governments supported Saddam Hussein both politically and financially through his worst excesses.

But why should poor AJ and his fellow soldiers be burdened with these details? It doesn't matter any more, does it? Hundreds of thousands of men, tanks, ships, choppers, bombs, ammunition, gas masks, high-protein food, whole aircrafts ferrying toilet paper, insect repellent, vitamins and bottled mineral water, are on the move. The phenomenal logistics of Operation Iraqi Freedom make it a universe unto itself. It doesn't need to justify its existence any more. It exists. It *is*.

President George W. Bush, Commander in Chief of the US Army, Navy, Air Force and Marines, has issued clear instructions: 'Iraq. Will. Be. Liberated'. (Perhaps he means that even if Iraqi people's bodies are killed, their souls will be liberated.) American and British citizens owe it to the Supreme Commander to forsake thought and rally behind their troops. Their countries are at war.

And what a war it is.

After using the 'good offices' of UN diplomacy (economic sanctions and weapons inspections) to ensure that Iraq was brought to its knees, its people starved, half a million of its children killed, its infrastructure severely damaged, *after making sure that most of its weapons have been destroyed*, in an act of cowardice that must surely be unrivalled in history, the 'Allies'/'Coalition of the Willing' (better known as the Coalition of the Bullied and Bought) – sent in an invading army!

Operation Iraqi Freedom? I don't think so. It's more like Operation Let's Run a Race, but First Let Me Break Your Knees.

So far the Iraqi army, with its hungry, ill-equipped soldiers, its old guns and ageing tanks, has somehow managed to temporarily confound and occasionally even out-manœuvre the 'Allies'. Faced with the richest, best-equipped, most powerful armed forces the world has ever seen, Iraq has shown spectacular courage and has even managed to put up what actually amounts to a *defence*. A defence which the Bush/Blair Pair have immediately denounced as deceitful and cowardly. (But then deceit is an old tradition with us natives. When we're invaded/colonized/occupied and stripped of all dignity, we turn to guile and opportunism.)

Even allowing for the fact that Iraq and the 'Allies' are at war, the extent to which the 'Allies' and their media cohorts are prepared to go is astounding to the point of being counter-productive to their own objectives.

When Saddam Hussein appeared on national TV to address the Iraqi people following the failure of the most elaborate assassination attempt in history – 'Operation Decapitation' – we had Geoff Hoon, British Defence Secretary deriding him for not having the courage to stand up and be killed, calling him a coward who hides in trenches. We then had a flurry of coalition speculation – Was it really Saddam Hussein, was it his double? Or was it Osama with a shave? Was it pre-recorded? Was it a speech? Was it black magic? Will it turn into a pumpkin if we really, really want it to?

After dropping not hundreds, but thousands of bombs on Baghdad, when a market-place was mistakenly blown up and civilians killed, a US army spokesman implied that the Iraqis were blowing themselves up! 'They're using very old stock. Their missiles go up and come down.'

If so, may we ask how this squares with the accusation that the Iraqi regime is a paid-up member of the Axis of Evil and a threat to world peace?

When the Arab TV station Al-Jazeera shows civilian casualties, it's denounced as 'emotive' Arab propaganda aimed at orchestrating hostility towards the 'Allies', as though Iraqis are dying only in order to make the 'Allies' look bad. Even French television has come in for some stick for similar reasons. But the awed, breathless footage of aircraft carriers, stealth bombers and cruise missiles arcing across the desert sky on American and British TV is described as the 'terrible beauty' of war.

When invading American soldiers (from the army 'that's only here to help') are taken prisoner and shown on Iraqi TV, George Bush says it violates the Geneva convention and 'exposes the evil at the heart of the regime'. But it is entirely acceptable for US television stations to show the hundreds of prisoners being held by the US government in Guantanamo Bay, kneeling on the ground with their hands tied behind their backs, blinded with opaque goggles and with earphones clamped on their ears, to ensure complete visual and aural deprivation. When questioned about the treatment of prisoners in Guantanamo Bay, US government officials don't deny that they're being ill-treated. They deny that they're 'prisoners of war'! They call them 'unlawful combatants', implying that their ill-treatment is legitimate! (So what's the Party Line on the massacre of prisoners in Mazar-e-Sharif, Afghanistan? Forgive and forget? And what of the prisoner tortured to death by the Special Forces at the Bagram Air Force Base? Doctors have formally called it homicide.)

When the 'Allies' bombed the Iraqi television station (also, incidentally, a contravention of the Geneva convention), there was vulgar jubilation in the American media. In fact, Fox TV had been lobbying for the attack for a while. It was seen as a righteous blow against Arab propaganda. But mainstream American and British TV continue to advertise themselves as 'balanced' when their propaganda has achieved hallucinatory levels.

Why should propaganda be the exclusive preserve of the western media? Just because they do it better?

Western journalists 'embedded' with troops are given the status of heroes reporting from the frontlines of war. Non-'embedded' journalists (like the BBC's Rageh Omaar, reporting from besieged and bombed Baghdad, witnessing, and clearly affected by, the sight of bodies of burned children and wounded people) are undermined even before they begin their report-age: 'We have to tell you that he is being monitored by the Iraqi Authorities.'

Increasingly, on British and American TV Iraqi sol-diers are being referred to as 'militia' (i.e.: rabble). One BBC correspondent portentously referred to them as 'quasi-terrorists'. Iraqi defence is 'resistance' or, worse still, 'pockets of resistance', Iraqi military strategy is deceit. (The US government bugging the phone lines of UN Security Council delegates, reported by the London *Observer*, is hard-headed prag-matism.) Clearly for the 'Allies', the only morally acceptable strategy the Iraqi army can pursue is to march out into the desert and be bombed by B-52s or be mowed down by machine-gun fire. Anything short of that is cheating.

And now we have the siege of Basra. About a million and a half people, 40 per cent of them children. Without clean water, and with very little food. We're still waiting for the legendary Shia 'uprising', for the happy hordes to stream out of the city and rain roses and hosannahs on the 'liberating' army. Where are the hordes? Don't they know that television productions work to tight schedules? (It may well be that if the Saddam Hussein regime falls there *will* be dancing on the streets the world over.)

After days of enforcing hunger and thirst on the citizens of Basra, the Allies have brought in a few trucks of food and water and positioned them tantalizingly on the outskirts of the city. Desperate people flock to the trucks and fight each other for food. (The water, we hear, is being *sold*. To revitalize the dying economy, you understand.) On top of the trucks, desperate photographers fought each other to get pictures of desperate people fighting each other for food. Those pictures will go out through photo agencies to newspapers and glossy magazines that pay extremely well. Their message: The messiahs are at hand, distributing fishes and loaves.

As of July last year, the delivery of 5.4 billion dollars' worth of supplies to Iraq was blocked by the Bush/

Blair Pair. It didn't really make the news. But now, under the loving caress of live TV, 450 tonnes of humanitarian aid – a miniscule fraction of what's actually needed (call it a script prop) – arrived on a British ship, the *Sir Galahad*. Its arrival in the port of Umm Qasr merited a whole day of live TV broadcasts. Barf bag, anyone?

Nick Guttmann, Head of Emergencies for Christian Aid, writing for the *Independent on Sunday*, said that it would take *thirty-two Sir Galahad*'s a *day* to match the amount of food Iraq was receiving before the bombing began.

We oughtn't to be surprised, though. It's old tactics. They've been at it for years. Remember this moderate proposal by John McNaughton from the Pentagon Papers published during the Vietnam War:

> *Strikes at population targets (per se) are likely not only to create a counterproductive wave of revulsion abroad and at home, but greatly to increase the risk of enlarging the war with China or the Soviet Union. Destruction of locks and dams, however – if handled right – might . . . offer promise. Such destruction does not kill or drown people. By shallow-flooding the rice, it leads after time to wide-spread starvation (more than a million?) unless*

> *food is provided – which we could offer to do 'at the conference table.'*

Times haven't changed very much. The technique has evolved into a doctrine. It's called 'Winning Hearts and Minds'.

■

So, here's the moral maths as it stands: Two hundred thousand Iraqis estimated to have been killed in the first Gulf War. Hundreds of thousands dead because of the economic sanctions. (At least that lot has been saved from Saddam Hussein.) More being killed every day. Tens of thousands of US soldiers who fought the 1991 war officially declared 'disabled' by a disease called the Gulf War Syndrome believed in part to be caused by exposure to depleted uranium. It hasn't stopped the 'Allies' from continuing to use depleted uranium.

And now this talk of bringing the UN back into the picture.

But that old UN girl – it turns out that she just ain't what she was cracked up to be. She's been demoted (although she retains her high salary). Now she's the world's janitor. She's the Filipino cleaning lady, the Indian jamadarni, the postal bride from Thailand, the Mexican household help, the Jamaican au pair. She's employed to clean other people's shit. She's used and abused at will.

Despite Tony Blair's earnest submissions, and all his fawning, George Bush has made it clear that the UN will play no independent part in the administration of post-war Iraq. The US will decide who gets those juicy 'reconstruction' contracts. But Bush has appealed to the international community not to 'politicize' the issue of humanitarian aid. On 28 March, after Bush called for the immediate resumption of the UN's Oil for Food programme, the UN Security Council voted unanimously for the resolution. This means that everybody agrees that Iraqi money (from the sale of Iraqi oil) should be used to feed Iraqi people who are starving because of US-led sanctions and the illegal US-led war.

Contracts for the 'reconstruction' of Iraq, we're told, in discussions on the business news, could jump-start the world economy. It's funny how the interests of American corporations are so often, so successfully and so deliberately confused with the interests of the world economy. While the American people will end up paying for the war, oil companies, weapons manufacturers, arms dealers, and corporations involved in 'reconstruction' work will make direct gains from the war. Many of them are old friends and former employers of the Bush/Cheney/Rumsfeld/Rice cabal. Bush has already asked Congress for 75 billion dollars. Contracts for 'reconstruction' are already being negotiated. The news doesn't hit the stands because much of the US corporate media is owned and managed by the same interests.

Operation Iraqi Freedom, Tony Blair assures us, is about returning Iraqi oil to the Iraqi people. That is, returning Iraqi oil to the Iraqi people via corporate multinationals. Like Shell, like Chevron, like Halliburton. Or are we missing the plot here? Perhaps Halliburton is actually an Iraqi company? Perhaps US Vice-President Dick Cheney (who was a former director of Halliburton) is a closet Iraqi?

As the rift between Europe and America deepens, there are signs that the world could be entering a new era of economic boycotts. CNN reported that Americans are emptying French wine into gutters, chanting 'We don't want your stinking wine'. We've heard about the re-baptism of French fries. Freedom fries they're called now. There's news trickling in about Americans boycotting German goods. The thing is that if the fallout of the war takes this turn, it is the US who will suffer the most. Its homeland may be defended by border patrols and nuclear weapons, but its economy is strung out across the globe. Its economic outposts are exposed and vulnerable to attack in every direction. Already the internet is buzzing with elaborate lists of American and British government products and companies that should be boycotted. Apart from the usual targets, Coke, Pepsi and McDonalds, government agencies like USAID, the British DFID, British and American banks, Arthur Anderson, Merrill Lynch, American Express, corporations like Bechtel and General Electric, and companies like Reebok, Nike and Gap could find themselves under siege. These lists are being honed and refined by activists across the world. They could become a practical guide that directs and channelizes the amorphous but growing fury in the world. Suddenly, the 'inevitablity' of the project of Corporate Globalization is beginning to sccm more than a little evitable.

It's become clear that the War against Terror is not really about terror, and the War on Iraq not only about oil. It's about a superpower's self-destructive impulse towards supremacy, stranglehold, global hegemony. The argument is being made that the people of Argentina and Iraq have both been decimated by the same process. Only the weapons used against them differ: In one case it's an IMF cheque book. In the other, cruise missiles.

Finally, there's the matter of Saddam Hussein's arsenal of Weapons of Mass Destruction. (Oops, nearly forgot about those!)

In the fog of war – one thing's for sure – if the Saddam Hussein regime indeed has Weapons of Mass Destruction, it is showing an astonishing degree of responsibility and restraint in the teeth of extreme provocation. Under similar circumstances, (say, if Iraqi troops were bombing New York and laying siege to Washington, DC) could we expect the same of the Bush regime? Would it keep its thousands of nuclear warheads in their wrapping paper? What about its chemical and biological weapons? Its stocks of anthrax, smallpox and nerve gas? Would it?

Excuse me while I laugh.

In the fog of war we're forced to speculate: Either Saddam Hussein is an extremely responsible tyrant. Or – he simply does not possess Weapons of Mass Destruction. Either way, regardless of what happens next, Iraq comes out of the argument smelling sweeter than the US government.

So here's Iraq – rogue state, grave threat to world peace, paid-up member of the Axis of Evil. Here's

Iraq, invaded, bombed, besieged, bullied, its sovereignty shat upon, its children killed by cancers, its
people blown up on the streets. And here's all of us
watching. CNN–BBC, BBC–CNN late into the night.
Here's all of us, enduring the horror of the war, enduring the horror of the propaganda and enduring the
slaughter of language as we know and understand it.
Freedom now means mass murder (or, in the US,
fried potatoes). When someone says 'humanitarian
aid' we automatically go looking for induced starvation. 'Embedded', I have to admit, is a great find.
It's what it sounds like. And what about 'arsenal of
tactics'? Nice!

In most parts of the world, the invasion of Iraq is
being seen as a racist war. The real danger of a racist
war unleashed by racist regimes is that it engenders
racism in everybody – perpetrators, victims, spec-
tators. It sets the parameters for the debate, it lays out
a grid for a particular way of thinking. There is a tidal
wave of hatred for the United States rising from the
ancient heart of the world. In Africa, Latin America,
Asia, Europe, Australia. I encounter it every day.
Sometimes it comes from the most unlikely sources.
Bankers, businessmen, yuppie students, and they
bring to it all the crassness of their conservative,
illiberal politics. That absurd inability to separate
governments from people: America is a nation of
morons, a nation of murderers, they say (with the

same carelessness with which they say, 'All Muslims are terrorists'). Even in the grotesque universe of racist insult, the British make their entry as add-ons. Arse-lickers, they're called.

Suddenly, I, who have been vilified for being 'anti-American' and 'anti-West', find myself in the extraordinary position of defending the people of America. And Britain.

Those who descend so easily into the pit of racist abuse would do well to remember the hundreds of thousands of American and British citizens who protested against their country's stockpile of nuclear weapons. And the thousands of American war resistors who forced their government to withdraw from Vietnam. They should know that the most scholarly, scathing, hilarious critiques of the US government and the 'American Way of Life' comes from American citizens. And that the funniest, most bitter condemnation of their prime minister comes from the British media. Finally, they should remember that right now, hundreds of thousands of British and American citizens are on the streets protesting the war. The Coalition of the Bullied and Bought consists of governments, not people. More than one third of America's citizens have survived the relentless propaganda they've been subjected to and many thousands are actively fighting their own government. In the ultra-patriotic climate that prevails in the US, that's as brave as any Iraqi fighting for his or her homeland.

While the 'Allies' wait in the desert for an uprising of Shia Muslims on the streets of Basra, the real uprising is taking place in hundreds of cities across the world. It has been the most spectacular display of public morality ever seen.

Most courageous of all are the hundreds of thousands of American people on the streets of America's great cities – Washington, New York, Chicago, San Francisco. The fact is that the only institution in the world today that is more powerful than the American government is American civil society. American citizens have a huge responsibility riding on their shoulders. How can we not salute and support those who not only acknowledge but act upon that responsibility? They are our allies, our friends.

■

At the end of it all, it remains to be said that dictators like Saddam Hussein, and all the other despots in the Middle-East, in the Central Asian Republics, in Africa and Latin America, many of them installed, supported and financed by the US government, are a menace to their own people. Other than strengthening the hand of civil society (instead of weakening it as has been done in the case of Iraq), there is no easy, pristine way of dealing with them. (It's odd how those who dismiss the peace movement as Utopian don't hesitate to proffer the most absurdly dreamy reasons for going to war: To stamp out terrorism, install democracy, eliminate fascism and, most entertainingly, to 'rid the world of evil-doers'.)

Regardless of what the propaganda machine tells us, these tin-pot dictators are not the greatest threat to the world. The real and pressing danger, the *greatest threat of all* is the locomotive force that drives the political and economic engine of the US government, currently piloted by George Bush. Bush-bashing is fun, because he makes such an easy, sumptuous target. It's true that he is a dangerous, almost suicidal pilot, but the machine he handles is far more danger-ous than the man himself.

Despite the pall of gloom that hangs over us today, I'd like to file a cautious plea for hope: In times of war, one wants one's weakest enemy at the helm of his forces. And President George W. Bush is certainly that. Any other even averagely intelligent US Presi-dent would have probably done the very same things, but would have managed to smoke up the glass and confuse the opposition. Perhaps even carry the UN with him. George Bush's tactless imprudence and his brazen belief that he can run the world with his riot squad has done the opposite. He has achieved what writers, activists and scholars have striven to achieve for decades. He has exposed the ducts. He has placed on full public view the working parts, the nuts and bolts of the apocalyptic apparatus of the American Empire.

Now that the blueprint (The Ordinary Person's Guide to Empire) has been put into mass circulation, it could be disabled quicker than the pundits predicted.

Bring on the spanners.

instant-mix imperial democracy
(buy one, get one free)

In these times when we have to race to keep abreast of the speed at which our freedoms are being snatched from us, and when few can afford the luxury of retreating from the streets for a while in order to return with an exquisite, fully formed political thesis replete with footnotes and references, what profound gift can I offer you tonight?

As we lurch from crisis to crisis, beamed directly into our brains by satellite TV, we have to think on our feet. On the move. We enter histories through the rubble of war. Ruined cities, parched fields, shrinking forests and dying rivers are our archives. Craters left by daisy cutters, our libraries.

So what can I offer you tonight? Some uncomfortable thoughts about money, war, empire, racism and democracy. Some worries that flit around my brain like a family of persistent moths that keep me awake at night.

Some of you will think it bad manners for a person like me, officially entered in the Big Book of Modern Nations as an 'Indian citizen', to come here and criticize the US government. Speaking for myself, I'm no flag-waver, no patriot, and am fully aware that venality, brutality, and hypocrisy are imprinted on the leaden soul of every state. But when a country ceases to be merely a country and becomes an empire, then the scale of operations changes dramatically. So may I clarify that tonight I speak as a subject of the American Empire? I speak as a slave who presumes to criticize her king.

Since lectures must be called something, mine tonight is called:

instant-mix imperial democracy
(buy one, get one free)

Way back in 1988, on 3 July, the USS *Vincennes*, a missile cruiser stationed in the Persian Gulf, accidentally shot down an Iranian airliner and killed 290 civilian passengers. George Bush the First, who was at the time on his presidential campaign, was asked to comment on the incident. He said quite subtly, 'I will never apologize for the United States. I don't care what the facts are.'

I don't care what the facts are. What a perfect maxim for the New American Empire. Perhaps a slight variation on the theme would be more apposite: *The facts can be whatever we want them to be.*

When the United States invaded Iraq, a *New York Times/CBS News* survey estimated that 42 per cent of the American public believed that Saddam Hussein was directly responsible for the September 11th attacks on the World Trade Center and the Pentagon. And an ABC news poll said that 55 per cent of Americans believed that Saddam Hussein directly supported Al Qaeda. None of this opinion is based on evidence (because there isn't any). All of it is based on insinuation, auto-suggestion and outright lies circulated by the US corporate media, otherwise known as the 'Free Press', that hollow pillar on which contemporary American democracy rests.

Public support in the US for the war against Iraq was founded on a multi-tiered edifice of falsehood and deceit, coordinated by the US government and faithfully amplified by the corporate media.

Apart from the invented links between Iraq and Al Qaeda, we had the manufactured frenzy about Iraq's Weapons of Mass Destruction. George Bush the Lesser went to the extent of saying it would be 'suicidal' for the US *not* to attack Iraq. We once again witnessed the paranoia that a starved, bombed, besieged country was about to annihilate almighty America. (Iraq was only the latest in a succession of countries – earlier there was Cuba, Nicaragua, Libya, Grenada, Panama). But this time it wasn't just your ordinary brand of friendly neighbourhood frenzy. It was Frenzy with a Purpose. It ushered in an old doctrine in a new bottle: the Doctrine of Pre-emptive Strike, a.k.a. The United States Can Do Whatever The Hell It Wants, And That's Official.

The war against Iraq has been fought and won and no Weapons of Mass Destruction have been found. Not even a little one. Perhaps they'll have to be planted before they're discovered. And then, the more troublesome amongst us will need an explanation for why Saddam Hussein didn't use them when his country was being invaded.

Of course, there'll be no answers. True Believers will make do with those fuzzy TV reports about the discovery of a few barrels of banned chemicals in an old shed. There seems to be no consensus yet about whether they're really chemicals; whether they're actually banned and whether the vessels they're contained in can technically be called barrels. (There were unconfirmed rumours that a teaspoonful of potassium permanganate and an old harmonica were found there too.)

Meanwhile, in passing, an ancient civilization has been casually decimated by a very recent, casually brutal nation.

Then there are those who say, so what if Iraq had no chemical and nuclear weapons? So what if there is no Al Qaeda connection? So what if Osama bin Laden hates Saddam Hussein as much as he hates the United States? Bush the Lesser has said Saddam Hussein was a 'Homicidal Dictator'.

And so, the reasoning goes, Iraq needed a 'regime change'.

■

Never mind that forty years ago, the CIA, under President John F. Kennedy, orchestrated a regime change in Baghdad. In 1963, after a successful coup, the Ba'ath party came to power in Iraq. Using lists provided by the CIA, the new Ba'ath regime systematically eliminated hundreds of doctors, teachers, lawyers and political figures known to be leftists. An entire intellectual community was slaughtered. (The same technique was used to massacre hundreds of thousands of people in Indonesia and East Timor.) The young Saddam Hussein was said to have had a hand in supervising the bloodbath. In 1979, after factional infighting within the Ba'ath Party, Saddam Hussein became the President of Iraq. In April 1980, while he was massacring Shias, the US National Security Adviser Zbigniew Brzezinski declared, 'We see no fundamental incompatibility of interests between the United States and Iraq.' Washington and London overtly and covertly supported Saddam Hussein. They financed him, equipped him, armed him and provided him with dual-use materials to manufacture weapons of mass destruction. They supported his worst excesses financially, materially and morally. They supported the eight-year war against

Iran and the 1988 gassing of Kurdish people in Halabja, crimes which fourteen years later were re-heated and served up as reasons to justify invading Iraq. After the first Gulf War, the 'Allies' fomented an uprising of Shias in Basra and then looked away while Saddam Hussein crushed the revolt and slaughtered thousands in an act of vengeful reprisal.

The point is, if Saddam Hussein was evil enough to merit the most elaborate, openly declared assassination attempt in history (the opening move of Operation Shock and Awe), then surely those who supported him ought at least to be tried for war crimes? Why aren't the faces of US and UK government officials on the infamous pack of cards of wanted men and women?

Because when it comes to Empire, facts don't matter.

Yes, but all that's in the past, we're told. Saddam Hussein is a monster who must be stopped *now*. And only the US can stop him. It's an effective technique, this use of the urgent morality of the present to obscure the diabolical sins of the past and the malevolent plans for the future. Indonesia, Panama, Nicaragua, Iraq, Afghanistan – the list goes on and on. Right now there are brutal regimes being groomed for the future – Egypt, Saudi Arabia, Turkey, Pakistan, the Central Asian Republics.

US Attorney General John Ashcroft recently declared that US freedoms are 'not the grant of any government or document, but . . . our endowment from God'. (Why bother with the United Nations when God himself is on hand?)

So here we are, the people of the world, confronted with an Empire armed with a mandate from heaven (*and*, as added insurance, the most formidable arsenal of weapons of mass destruction in history). Here we arc, confronted with an Empire that has conferred upon itself the right to go to war at will, and the right to deliver people from corrupting ideologies, from religious fundamentalists, dictators, sexism, and poverty by the age-old, tried-and-tested practice of extermination. Empirc is on the move, and Democracy is its sly new war cry. Democracy, home-delivered to your doorstep by daisy-cutters. Death is a small price for people to pay for the privilege of sampling this new product: Instant-Mix Imperial Democracy (bring to a boil, add oil, then bomb).

But then perhaps chinks, negroes, dinks, gooks and wogs don't really qualify as real people. Perhaps our deaths don't qualify as real deaths. Our histories don't qualify as history. They never have.

Speaking of history, in these past months, while the world watched, the US invasion and occupation of

Iraq was broadcast on live TV. Like Osama bin Laden and the Taliban in Afghanistan, the regime of Saddam Hussein simply disappeared. This was followed by what analysts called a 'power vacuum'. Cities that had been under siege, without food, water and electricity for days, cities that had been bombed relentlessly, people who had been starved and systematically impoverished by the UN sanctions regime for more than a decade, were suddenly left with no semblance of urban administration. A seven-thousand-year-old civilization slid into anarchy. On live TV.

Vandals plundered shops, offices, hotels and hospitals. American and British soldiers stood by and watched. They said they had no orders to act. In effect, they had orders to kill people, but not to protect them. Their priorities were clear. The safety and security of Iraqi people was not their business. The security of whatever little remained of Iraq's infrastructure was not their business. But the security and safety of Iraq's oil fields were. Of course they were. The oil fields were 'secured' almost before the invasion began.

On CNN and the BBC the scenes of the rampage were played and replayed. TV commentators, army and government spokespersons portrayed it as a 'liberated people' venting their rage at a despotic regime. US Defence Secretary Donald Rumsfeld said: 'It's untidy. Freedom's untidy and free people are free to commit crimes and make mistakes and do bad things.' Did anybody know that Donald Rumsfeld was an anarch- ist? I wonder – did he hold the same view during the riots in Los Angeles following the beating of Rodney King? Would he care to share his thesis about the Untidiness of Freedom with the two million people being held in US prisons right now? (The world's 'freest' country has the highest number of prisoners in the world.) Would he discuss its merits with young African American men, 28 per cent of whom will spend some part of their adult lives in jail? Could he explain why he serves under a president who oversaw 152 executions when he was governor of Texas?

Before the war on Iraq began, the Office of Recon- struction and Humanitarian Assistance (ORHA) sent the Pentagon a list of sixteen crucial sites to protect. The National Museum was second on that list. Yet the Museum was not just looted, it was desecrated. It was a repository of an ancient cultural heritage. Iraq as we know it today was part of the river valley of Mesopotamia. The civilization that grew along the banks of the Tigris and the Euphrates produced the world's first writing, first calendar, first library, first city, and, yes, the world's first democracy. King Hammurabi of Babylon was the first to codify laws governing the social life of citizens. It was a code in which abandoned women, prostitutes, slaves, and even animals had rights. The Hammurabi code is acknowledged not just as the birth of legality, but the beginning of an understanding of the concept of social justice. The US government could not have chosen a more inappropriate land in which to stage its illegal war and display its grotesque disregard for justice.

At a Pentagon briefing during the days of looting, Secretary Rumsfeld, Prince of Darkness, turned on his media cohorts who had served him so loyally through the war. 'The images you are seeing on television, you are seeing over and over and over, and it's the same picture, of some person walking out of some building with a vase, and you see it twenty times and you say, "My God, were there that many vases? Is it possible that there were that many vases in the whole country?"'

Laughter rippled through the press room. Would it be all right for the poor of Harlem to loot the Metropolitan Museum? Would it be greeted with similar mirth?

The last building on the ORHA list of sixteen sites to be protected was the Ministry of Oil. It was the only one that was given protection. Perhaps the occupying army thought that in Muslim countries lists are read upside-down?

Television tells us that Iraq has been 'liberated' and that Afghanistan is well on its way to becoming a paradise for women – thanks to Bush and Blair, the twenty-first century's leading feminists. In reality, Iraq's infrastructure has been destroyed. Its people brought to the brink of starvation. Its food stocks depleted. And its cities devastated by a complete administrative breakdown. Iraq is being ushered in the direction of a civil war between Shias and Sunnis. Meanwhile, Afghanistan has lapsed back into the pre-Taliban era of anarchy, and its territory has been carved up into fiefdoms by hostile warlords.

Undaunted by all this, on 2 May Bush the Lesser launched his 2004 campaign hoping to be finally elected US President. In what probably constitutes the shortest flight in history, a military jet landed on an aircraft carrier, the USS *Abraham Lincoln*, which was so close to shore that, according to the Associated Press, administration officials acknowledged 'positioning the massive ship to provide the best TV angle for Bush's speech, with the sea as his background instead of the San Diego coastline'. President Bush, who never served his term in the military, emerged from the cockpit in fancy dress – a US military bomber jacket, combat boots, flying goggles, helmet. Waving to his cheering troops, he officially proclaimed victory over Iraq. He was careful to say that it was 'just one victory in a war on terror . . . [which] still goes on'.

It was important to avoid making a straightforward victory announcement, because under the Geneva Convention a victorious army is bound by legal obligations of an occupying force, a responsibility that the Bush administration does not want to burden itself with. Also, closer to the 2004 elections, in order to woo wavering voters, another victory in the 'War on Terror' might become necessary. Syria is being fattened for the kill.

It was Herman Goering, that old Nazi, who said 'People can always be brought to the bidding of the leaders . . . All you have to do is tell them they're being attacked and denounce the pacifists for a lack of patriotism and exposing the country to danger. It works the same way in any country.'

He's right. It's dead easy. That's what the Bush regime banks on. The distinction between election campaigns and war, between democracy and oligarchy, seems to be closing fast.

The only caveat in these campaign wars is that US lives must not be lost. It shakes voter confidence. But the problem of US soldiers being killed in combat has been licked. More or less.

At a media briefing before 'Operation Shock and Awe' was unleashed, General Tommy Franks announced,

'This campaign will be like no other in history.' Maybe he's right.

I'm no military historian, but when was the last time a war was fought like this?

As soon as the war began, the governments of France, Germany and Russia, which refused to allow a final resolution legitimizing the war to be passed in the UN Security Council, fell over each other to say how much they wanted the United States to win. President Jacques Chirac offered French airspace to the Anglo-American air force. US military bases in Germany were open for business. German Foreign Minister Joschka Fischer publicly hoped for the 'rapid collapse' of the Saddam Hussein regime. Vladimir Putin publicly hoped for the same. These are governments that colluded in the enforced disarming of Iraq before their dastardly rush to take the side of those who attacked it. Apart from hoping to share the spoils, they hoped Empire would honour their pre-war oil contracts with Iraq. Only the very naïve could expect old Imperialists to behave otherwise.

Leaving aside the cheap thrills and the lofty moral speeches made in the UN during the run-up to the war, eventually, at the moment of crisis, the unity of Western governments – despite the opposition from the majority of their people – was overwhelming.

When the Turkish government temporarily bowed to the views of 90 per cent of its population, and turned down the US government's offer of billions of dollars of blood money for the use of Turkish soil, it was accused of lacking 'democratic principles'. According to a Gallup International poll, in no European country was support for a war carried out 'unilaterally by America and its allies' higher than 11 per cent. But the governments of England, Italy, Spain, Hungary and other countries of Eastern Europe were praised for disregarding the views of the majority of their people and supporting the illegal invasion. That, presumably, was fully in keeping with democratic principles. What's it called? New Democracy? (Like Britain's New Labour?)

In stark contrast to the venality displayed by their governments, on 15 February, weeks before the invasion, in the most spectacular display of public morality the world has ever seen, more than 10 million people marched against the war on five continents. Many of you, I'm sure, were among them. They – *we* – were disregarded with utter disdain. When asked to react to the anti-war demonstrations, President Bush said, 'It's like deciding, well, I'm going to decide policy based upon a focus group. The role of a leader is to decide policy based upon the security, in this case the security of the people.'

Democracy, the modern world's holy cow, is in crisis. And the crisis is a profound one. Every kind of outrage is being committed in the name of democracy. It has become little more than a hollow word, a pretty shell, emptied of all content or meaning. It can be whatever you want it to be. Democracy is the Free World's whore, willing to dress up, dress down, willing to satisfy a whole range of tastes, available to be used and abused at will.

Until quite recently, right up to the 1980s, democracy did seem as though it might actually succeed in delivering a degree of real social justice.

But modern democracies have been around for long enough for neo-liberal capitalists to learn how to subvert them. They have mastered the technique of infiltrating the instruments of democracy – the 'independent' judiciary, the 'free' press, the parliament – and moulding them to their purpose. The project of corporate globalization has cracked the code. Free elections, a free press and an independent judiciary mean little when the free market has reduced them to commodities on sale to the highest bidder.

To fully comprehend the extent to which Democracy is under siege, it might be an idea to look at what goes on in some of our contemporary democracies. The world's largest: India, (which I have written about at some length and therefore will not speak about tonight). The world's most interesting: South Africa. The world's most powerful: the USA. And, most instructive of all, the plans that are being made to usher in the world's newest: Iraq.

In South Africa, after 300 years of brutal domination of the black majority by a white minority through colonialism and apartheid, a non-racial, multi-party democracy came to power in 1994. It was a phenomenal achievement. Within two years of coming to power, the African National Congress had genuflected with no caveats to the Market God. Its massive programme of structural adjustment, privatization and liberalization has only increased the hideous disparities between the rich and the poor. More than a million people have lost their jobs. The corporatization of basic services – electricity, water and housing – has meant that 10 million South Africans, almost a quarter of the population, has been disconnected from water and electricity. Two million have been evicted from their homes.

Meanwhile, a small white minority that has been historically privileged by centuries of brutal exploitation are more secure than ever before. They continue to control the land, the farms, the factories and the abundant natural resources of that country. For them, the transition from apartheid to neo-liberalism barely

disturbed the grass. It's apartheid with a clean conscience. And it goes by the name of Democracy.

Democracy has become Empire's euphemism for neo-
liberal capitalism.

In countries of the first world, too, the machinery of
democracy has been effectively subverted. Politicians,
media barons, judges, powerful corporate lobbies and
government officials are imbricated in an elaborate
underhand configuration that completely undermines
the lateral arrangement of checks and balances between the constitution, courts of law, parliament, the
administration and, perhaps most important of all, the
independent media that form the structural basis of
a parliamentary democracy. Increasingly, the imbrica-
tion is neither subtle nor elaborate.

Italian Prime Minister Silvio Berlusconi, for instance,
has a controlling interest in major Italian newspapers,
magazines, television channels and publishing houses.
The *Financial Times* reported that he controls about
90 per cent of Italy's TV viewership. Recently, during
a trial on bribery charges, while insisting he was the
only person who could save Italy from the left, he
said, 'How much longer do I have to keep living this
life of sacrifices?' That bodes ill for the remaining 10
per cent of Italy's TV viewership. What price Free
Speech? Free Speech for *whom*?

In the United States, the arrangement is more complex. Clear Channel Worldwide Incorporated is the largest radio station owner in the country. It runs more than 1,200 channels, which together account for 9 per cent of the market. Its CEO contributed hundreds of thousands of dollars to Bush's election campaign. When hundreds of thousands of American citizens took to the streets to protest against the war on Iraq, Clear Channel organized pro-war patriotic 'Rallies for America' across the country. It used its radio stations to advertise the events and then sent correspondents to cover them as though they were breaking news. The era of manufacturing consent has given way to the era of manufacturing news. Soon media newsrooms will drop the pretence, and start hiring theatre directors instead of journalists.

As America's show business gets more and more violent and war-like, and America's wars get more and more like show business, some interesting cross-overs are taking place. The designer who built the 250,000 dollar set in Qatar from which General Tommy Franks stage-managed news coverage of Operation Shock and Awe also built sets for Disney, MGM and *Good Morning America*.

It is a cruel irony that the US, which has the most ardent, vociferous defenders of the idea of Free Speech, and (until recently) the most elaborate legislation to protect it, has so circumscribed the space in which that freedom can be expressed. In a strange, convoluted way, the sound and fury that accompanies the legal and *conceptual* defence of Free Speech in America serves to mask the process of the rapid erosion of the possibilities of actually *exercising* that freedom.

The news and entertainment industry in the US is for the most part controlled by a few major corporations – AOL-Time Warner, Disney, Viacom, News Corporation. Each of these corporations owns and controls TV stations, film studios, record companies and publishing ventures. Effectively, the exits are sealed.

America's media empire is controlled by a tiny coterie of people. Chairman of the Federal Communications Commission Michael Powell, the son of Secretary of State Colin Powell, has proposed even further deregulation of the communication industry, which will lead to even greater consolidation.

■

So here it is – the world's greatest democracy, led by a man who was not legally elected. America's Supreme Court gifted him his job. What price have American people paid for this spurious presidency?

In the three years of George Bush the Lesser's term, the American economy has lost more than 2 million jobs. Outlandish military expenses, corporate welfare and tax giveaways to the rich have created a financial crisis for the US educational system. According to a survey by the National Council of State Legislatures, US states cut 49 billion dollars in public services, health, welfare benefits and education in 2002. They plan to cut another 25.7 billion dollars this year. That makes a total of 75 billion dollars. Bush's initial budget request to Congress to finance the war in Iraq was 80 billion dollars.

So who's paying for the war? America's poor. Its students, its unemployed, its single mothers, its hospital and home-care patients, its teachers and health workers.

And who's actually fighting the war?

Once again, America's poor. The soldiers who are baking in Iraq's desert sun are not the children of the rich. Only one of all the representatives in Congress and the Senate has a child fighting in Iraq. America's 'volunteer' army in fact depends on a poverty draft of poor whites, Blacks, Latinos and Asians looking for a way to earn a living and get an education. Federal statistics show that African Americans make up 21 per cent of the total armed forces and 29 per cent of the US army. They count for only 12 per cent of the general population. It's ironic, isn't it – the disproportionately high representation of African Americans in the army and prison? Perhaps we should take a positive view, and look at this as affirmative action at its most effective. Nearly 4 million Americans (2 per cent of the population) have lost the right to vote because of felony convictions. Of that number, 1.4 million are African Americans, which means that 13 per cent of all voting-age Black people have been disenfranchised.

For African Americans there's also affirmative action in death. A study by the economist Amartya Sen shows that African Americans as a group have a lower life expectancy than people born in China, in the Indian State of Kerala (where I come from), Sri Lanka or Costa Rica. Bangladeshi men have a better chance of making it to the age of forty than African American men from here in Harlem.

This year, on what would have been Martin Luther King Jr.'s seventy-fourth birthday, President Bush denounced the University of Michigan's affirmative action programme favouring Blacks and Latinos. He called it 'divisive', 'unfair' and 'unconstitutional'. The successful effort to keep Blacks off the voting rolls in the State of Florida in order that George Bush be elected was of course neither unfair nor unconstitutional. I don't suppose affirmative action for White Boys From Yale ever is.

So we know who's paying for the war. We know who's fighting it. But who will benefit from it? Who is homing in on the reconstruction contracts estimated to be worth up to one hundred billion dollars? Could it be America's poor and unemployed and sick? Could it be America's single mothers? Or America's Black and Latino minorities?

Operation Iraqi Freedom, George Bush assures us, is about returning Iraqi oil to the Iraqi people. That is, returning Iraqi oil to the Iraqi people via corporate multinationals. Like Bechtel, like Chevron, like Halliburton.

Once again it is a small, tight circle that connects corporate, military, and government leadership to one another. The promiscuousness, the cross-pollination is outrageous.

Consider this: The Defense Policy Board is a government-appointed group that advised the Pentagon on defense policy. Its members are appointed by the Under Secretary of Defense and approved by Donald Rumsfeld. Its meetings are classified. No information is available for public scrutiny.

The Washington-based Centre for Public Integrity found that nine out of the thirty members of the Defense Policy Board are connected to companies that were awarded defence contracts worth 76 billion dollars between the years 2001 and 2002. One of them, Jack Sheehan, a retired marine corps general, is a senior vice president at Bechtel, the giant international engineering outfit. Riley Bechtel, the company chairman, is on the President's Export Council. Former Secretary of State George Schultz, who is also on the board of directors of the Bechtel Group, is the chairman of the advisory board of the Committee for the Liberation of Iraq. When asked by the *New York Times* whether he was concerned about the appearance of a conflict of interest, he said, 'I don't know that Bechtel would particularly benefit from it. But if there's work to be done, Bechtel is the type of company that could do it.'

Bechtel has been awarded a 680 million dollar reconstruction contract in Iraq. According to the Centre for Responsive Politics, Bechtel contributed 1.3 million dollars towards the 1999–2000 Republican Campaign.

■

Arcing across this subterfuge, dwarfing it by the sheer magnitude of its malevolence, is America's anti-terrorism legislation. The USA Patriot Act, passed on 13 October 2001, has become the blueprint for similar anti-terrorism bills in countries across the world. It was passed in the House of Representatives by a majority vote of 337 to 79. According to the *New York Times*, 'Many lawmakers said it had been impossible to truly debate, or even read, the legislation.'

The Patriot Act ushers in an era of systemic automated surveillance. It gives the government the authority to monitor phones and computers and spy on people in ways that would have seemed completely unacceptable a few years ago. It gives the FBI the power to seize all of the circulation, purchasing and other records of library users and bookstore customers on the suspicion that they are part of a terrorist network. It blurs the boundaries between speech and criminal activity, creating the space to construe acts of civil disobedience as violating the law.

Already hundreds of people are being held indefinitely as 'unlawful combatants'. (In India, the number is in the thousands. In Israel, 5,000 Palestinians are now being detained). Non-citizens, of course, have no rights at all. They can simply be 'disappeared' like the people of Chile under Washington's old ally, General Pinochet. More than one thousand people, many of them Muslim or of Middle Eastern origin, have been detained, some without access to legal representatives.

■

Apart from paying the actual economic costs of war, American people are paying for these wars of 'liberation' with their own freedoms. For the ordinary American, the price of 'New Democracy' in other countries is the death of real democracy at home.

Meanwhile, Iraq is being groomed for 'liberation'. (Or did they mean 'liberalization' all along?) The *Wall Street Journal* reports that 'the Bush administration has drafted sweeping plans to remake Iraq's economy in the U.S. image'.

Iraq's constitution is being redrafted. Its trade laws, tax laws and intellectual property laws rewritten in order to turn it into an American-style capitalist economy.

The United States Agency for International Development has invited US companies to bid for contracts that range from road building and water systems to textbook distribution, and cell phone networks.

Soon after Bush the Second announced that he wanted American farmers to feed the world, Dam Amstutz, a former senior executive of Cargill, the biggest grain exporter in the world, was put in charge of agricultural reconstruction in Iraq. Kevin Watkin, Oxfam's policy director, said, 'Putting Dam Amstutz in charge of agricultural reconstruction in Iraq is like putting Saddam Hussein in the chair of a human rights commission.'

The two men who have been shortlisted to run operations for managing Iraqi oil have worked with Shell, BP and Fluer. Fluer is embroiled in a lawsuit by black South African workers who have accused the company of exploiting and brutalizing them during the apartheid era. Shell, of course, is well known for its devastation of the Ogoni tribal lands in Nigeria.

Tom Brokaw (one of America's best-known TV anchors) was inadvertently succinct about the process. 'One of the things we don't want to do' he said, 'is to destroy the infrastructure of Iraq because in a few days we're going to own that country.'

Now that the ownership deeds are being settled, Iraq is ready for New Democracy.

So, as Lenin used to ask: What Is To Be Done?

Well . . .

We might as well accept the fact that there is no conventional military force that can successfully challenge the American war machine. Terrorist strikes only give the US Government an opportunity that it is eagerly awaiting to further tighten its stranglehold. Within days of an attack you can bet that Patriot II would be passed. To argue against US military aggression by saying that it will increase the possibilities of terrorist strikes is futile. It's like threatening Brer Rabbit that you'll throw him into the bramble bush. Anybody who has read the document called 'The Project for the New American Century' can attest to that. The government's suppression of the Congressional Committee Report on September 11th, which found that there was intelligence warning of the strikes that was ignored, also attests to the fact that, for all their posturing, the terrorists and the Bush regime might as well be working as a team. They both hold people responsible for the actions of their governments. They both believe in the doctrine of collective guilt and collective punishment. Their actions benefit each other greatly.

The US government has already displayed in no uncertain terms the range and extent of its capability for paranoid aggression. In human psychology, paranoid aggression is usually an indicator of nervous insecurity. It could be argued that it's no different in the case of the psychology of nations. Empire is paranoid because it has a soft underbelly.

Its homeland may be defended by border patrols and nuclear weapons, but its economy is strung out across the globe. Its economic outposts are exposed and vulnerable.

Yet, it would be naïve to imagine that we can directly confront Empire. Our strategy must be to isolate Empire's working parts and disable them one by one. No target is too small. No victory too insignificant. We could reverse the idea of the economic sanctions imposed on poor countries by Empire and its Allies. We could impose a regime of Peoples' Sanctions on every corporate house that has been awarded with a contract in post-war Iraq, just as activists in this country and around the world targeted institutions of apartheid. Each one of them should be named, exposed and boycotted. Forced out of business. That could be our response to the Shock and Awe campaign. It would be a great beginning.

Another urgent challenge is to expose the corporate media for the boardroom bulletin that it really is. We need to create a universe of alternative information. We need to support independent media like Democracy Now, Alternative Radio, South End Press.

The battle to reclaim democracy is going to be a difficult one. Our freedoms were not granted to us by any governments. They were wrested *from* them by us.

And once we surrender them, the battle to retrieve them is called a revolution. It is a battle that must range across continents and countries. It must not acknowledge national boundaries, but, if it is to succeed, has to begin here. In America. The only institution more powerful than the US government is American civil society. The rest of us are subjects of slave nations. We are by no means powerless, but you have the power of proximity. You have access to the Imperial Palace and the Emperor's chambers. Empire's conquests are being carried out in your name, and you have the right to refuse. You could refuse to fight. Refuse to move those missiles from the warehouse to the dock. Refuse to wave that flag. Refuse the victory parade.

You have a rich tradition of resistance. You need only read Howard Zinn's *A People's History of the United States* to remind yourself of this.

Hundreds of thousands of you have survived the relentless propaganda you have been subjected to, and are actively fighting your own government. In the ultra-patriotic climate that prevails in the United States, that's as brave as any Iraqi or Afghan or Palestinian fighting for his or her homeland.

If you join the battle, not in your hundreds of thousands, but in your millions, you will be greeted joyously by the rest of the world. And you will see how beautiful it is to be gentle instead of brutal, safe instead of scared. Befriended instead of isolated. Loved instead of hated.

I hate to disagree with your president. Yours is by no means a great nation. But you could be a great people.

History is giving you the chance.

Seize the time.

when the saints go marching out
the strange fate of martin, mohandas and mandela

when the saints go marching out
the strange fate of martin, mohandas and mandela

We're coming up to the fortieth anniversary of the March on Washington, when Martin Luther King gave his famous 'I have a dream' speech. Perhaps it's time to reflect – again – on what has become of that dream.

It's interesting how icons, when their time has passed, are commodified and appropriated (some voluntarily, others involuntarily) to promote the prejudice, bigotry and inequity they battled against. But then in an age when everything's up for sale, why not icons? In an era when all of humanity, when every creature of God's earth, is trapped between the IMF cheque book and the American cruise missile, can icons stage a getaway?

Martin Luther King is part of a trinity. So it's hard to think of him without two others elbowing their way into the picture: Mohandas Gandhi and Nelson Mandela. The three high priests of non-violent resistance. Together they represent (to a greater or lesser extent) the twentieth century's non-violent liberation struggles (or should we say 'negotiated settlements'?): of colonized against colonizer, former slave against slave owner.

Today the elites of the very societies and peoples in whose name the battles for freedom were waged use them as mascots to entice new masters.

Mohandas, Mandela, Martin.
India, South Africa, the United States.
Broken dreams, betrayal, nightmares.
A quick snapshot of the supposedly 'Free World' today.

Last March in India, in Gujarat – *Gandhi*'s Gujarat – right-wing Hindu mobs murdered 2,000 Muslims in a chillingly efficient orgy of violence. Women were gang-raped and burned alive. Muslim tombs and shrines were razed to the ground. More than a hundred and fifty thousand Muslims have been driven from their homes. The economic base of the community has been destroyed. Eye-witness accounts and several fact-finding commissions have accused the state government and the police of collusion in the violence. I was present at a meeting where a group of victims kept wailing, 'Please save us from the police! That's all we ask . . .'

In December 2002, the same state government was voted back to office. Narendra Modi, who was widely accused of having orchestrated the riots, has embarked on his second term as Chief Minister of Gujarat. On 15 August, Independence Day, he hoisted the Indian flag before thousands of cheering people. In a gesture of menacing symbolism, he wore the black RSS cap – which proclaims him as a member of the Hindu nationalist guild that has not been shy of admiring Hitler and his methods.

One hundred and thirty million Muslims – not to mention the other minorities, Dalits, Christians, Sikhs, Adivasis – live in India under the shadow of Hindu nationalism.

As his confidence in his political future brimmed over, Narendra Modi, master of seizing the political moment, invited Nelson Mandela to Gujarat to be the Chief Guest at the celebration of Gandhi's birth anniversary on 2 October. Fortunately the invitation was turned down.

And what of Mandela's South Africa? Otherwise known as the Small Miracle, the Rainbow Nation of God? South Africans say that the only miracle they know of is how quickly the rainbow has been privatised, sectioned off and auctioned to the highest bidders. Within two years of taking office in 1994, the

African National Congress genuflected with hardly a caveat to the Market God. In its rush to replace Argentina as neo-liberalism's poster boy, it has instituted a massive programme of privatization and structural adjustment. The government's promise to redistribute agricultural land to 26 million landless people has remained in the realm of dark humour. While 60 per cent of the population remains landless, almost all agricultural land is owned by 60,000 white farmers. (Small wonder that George Bush on his recent visit to South Africa referred to Thabo Mbeki as his 'point man' on the Zimbabwe issue.)

Post-apartheid, the income of 40 per cent of the poorest Black families has diminished by about 20 per cent. Two million have been evicted from their homes. 600 die of AIDS every day. Forty per cent of the population is unemployed and that number is rising sharply. The corporatization of basic services has meant that millions have been disconnected from water and electricity.

A fortnight ago, I visited the home of Teresa Naidoo in Chatsworth, Durban. Her husband had died the previous day of AIDS. She had no money for a coffin. She and her two small children are HIV-positive. The government disconnected her water supply because she was unable to pay her water bills and her rent arrears for her tiny council flat. The government dismisses her troubles and those of millions like her as a 'culture of non-payment'.

In what ought to be an international scandal, this same government has officially asked the judge in a US court case to rule *against* forcing companies to pay reparations for the role they played during apartheid. Its reasoning is that reparations – in other words, justice – will discourage foreign investment. So South Africa's poorest must pay apartheid's debts, so that those who amassed profit by exploiting Black people during apartheid can profit even more from the goodwill generated by Nelson Mandela's Rainbow Nation of God. President Thabo Mbeki is still called 'comrade' by his colleagues in government. In South Africa, Orwellian parody goes under the genre of Real Life.

What's left to say about Martin Luther King's America? Perhaps it's worth asking a simple question: had he been alive today, would he have chosen to stay warm in his undisputed place in the pantheon of Great Americans? Or would he have stepped off his pedestal, shrugged off the empty hosannas and walked out on to the streets to rally his people once more?

On 4 April 1967, one year before he was assassinated, Martin Luther King spoke at the Riverside Church in

New York City. That evening he said: 'I could never again raise my voice against the violence of the oppressed in the ghettos without having first spoken clearly to the greatest purveyor of violence in the world today – my own government.'

Has anything happened in the thirty-six years between 1967 and 2003 that would have made him change his mind? Or would he be doubly confirmed in his opinion after the overt and covert wars and acts of mass killing that successive governments of his country, both Republican and Democrat, have engaged in since then?

Let's not forget that Martin Luther King Jr. didn't start out as a militant. He began as a Persuader, a Believer. In 1964 he won the Nobel Peace Prize. He was held up by the media as an exemplary Black leader, unlike, say, the more militant Malcolm X. It was only three years later that Martin Luther King publicly connected the US government's racist war in Vietnam with its racist policies at home.

In 1967, in an uncompromising, militant speech, he denounced the American invasion of Vietnam. He said: 'We have repeatedly been faced with the cruel irony of watching Negro and white boys on TV screens as they kill and die together for a nation that has been unable to seat them together in the same schools. So we watch them in brutal solidarity burning the huts of a poor village, but we realize they would hardly live on the same block in Chicago.'

The *New York Times* had some wonderful counter-logic to offer the growing anti-war sentiment among Black Americans: 'In Vietnam,' it said, 'the Negro for the first time has been given the chance to do his share of fighting for his country.'

It omitted to mention Martin Luther King's remark that '[t]here are twice as many Negroes dying in Vietnam as whites in proportion to their size in the population'. It omitted to mention that when the body bags came home, some of the Black soldiers were buried in segregated graves in the deep South.

What would Martin Luther King Jr. say today about the fact that federal statistics show that African Americans, who count for 12 per cent of America's population, make up 21 per cent of the total armed forces and 29 per cent of the US army?

Perhaps he would take a positive view and look at this as affirmative action at its most effective?

What would he say about the fact that having fought so hard to win the right to vote, today 1.4 million African Americans, which means 13 per cent of all voting-age Black people, have been disenfranchised because of felony convictions?

But the most pertinent question of all is: what would Martin Luther King Jr. say to those Black men and women who make up a fifth of America's armed forces and close to a third of the US army?

To Black soldiers fighting in Vietnam, Martin Luther King Jr. said, 'as we counsel young men concerning military service we must clarify for them our nation's role in Vietnam and challenge them with the alternative of conscientious objection'.

In April 1967, at a massive anti-war demonstration in Manhattan, Stokely Carmichael described the draft as 'White people sending Black people to make war on yellow people in order to defend land they stole from red people'.

What's changed? Except of course the compulsory draft has become a poverty draft – a different kind of compulsion.

Would Martin Luther King say today that the invasion and occupation of Iraq and Afghanistan are in any way morally different from the US government's invasion of Vietnam? Would he say that it was just and moral to participate in these wars? Would he say that it was right for the US government to have supported a dictator like Saddam Hussein politically and financially for years while he committed his worst excesses against Kurds, Iranians and Iraqis in the 1980s when he was an ally against Iran?

And that when that dictator began to chafe at the bit, as Saddam Hussein did, would he say it was right to go to war against Iraq, to fire several hundred tonnes of depleted uranium into its fields, to degrade its water supply systems, to institute a regime of economic sanctions that resulted in the death of half a million children, to use UN weapons inspectors to force it to disarm, to mislead the public about an arsenal of weapons of mass destruction that could be deployed in a matter of minutes, and then, when the country was on its knees, to send in an invading army to conquer it, occupy it, humiliate its people, take control of its natural resources and infrastructure, and award contracts worth hundreds of millions of dollars to American corporations like Bechtel?

When he spoke out against the Vietnam War, Martin Luther King drew some connections that many these days shy away from making. He said, 'The problem of racism, the problem of economic exploitation, and the problem of war are all tied together. These are the triple evils that are inter-related.' Would he tell people today that it is right for the US government to export its cruelties – its racism, its economic bullying and its war machine to poorer countries?

Would he say that Black Americans must fight for their fair share of the American pie and the bigger the pie, the better their share – never mind the terrible price that the people of Africa, Asia, the Middle East and Latin America are paying for the American Way of Life? Would he support the grafting of the Great American Dream on to his own dream, which was a very different, very beautiful sort of dream? Or would he see that as a desecration of his memory and everything that he stood for?

The Black American struggle for civil rights gave us some of the most magnificent political fighters, thinkers, public speakers and writers of our times. Martin Luther King Jr., Malcolm X, Fannie Lou Hamer, Ella Baker, James Baldwin, and of course the marvellous, magical, mythical Muhammad Ali.

Who has inherited their mantle?

Could it be the likes of Colin Powell? Condoleezza Rice? Michael Powell?

They're the exact opposite of icons or role models. They *appear* to be the embodiment of Black people's dreams of material success, but in actual fact they represent the Great Betrayal. They are the liveried doormen guarding the portals of the glittering ballroom against the press and swirl of the darker races. Their role and purpose is to be trotted out by the Bush administration looking for brownie points in its racist wars and African safaris.

If these are Black America's new icons, then the old ones must be dispensed with because they do not belong in the same pantheon. If these are Black America's new icons, then perhaps the haunting image that Mike Marqusee describes in his beautiful book *Redemption Song* – an old Muhammad Ali afflicted with Parkinson's disease, advertising a retirement pension – symbolizes what has happened to Black Power, not just in the United States but the world over.

If Black America genuinely wishes to pay homage to its real heroes, and to all those unsung people who fought by their side, if the world wishes to pay homage, then it's time to march on Washington. Again. Keeping hope alive – for all of us.

(This is the text for a fifteen-minute radio essay broadcast by BBC Radio 4, on 25 August 2003. In this version, direct quotations have been used. The BBC determined it was legally obliged to use only paraphrases of King's words because of copyright restrictions on the use of King's public speeches.)

notes

ahimsa

[1] The government of India plans to build thirty large, 135 medium, and 3,000 small dams on the Narmada to generate electricity, displacing 400,000 people in the process. For more information, see http://www.narmada.org.

[2] See http://www.jang.com.pk/thenews/spedition/pak-india/accord.htm.

[3] The activists ended their fast on 18 June 2002 after an independent committee was set up to look into the issue of resettlement. For more information, see http://www.narmada.org/nba-press-releases;jun-2002/fast.ends.html.

come september

[1] See John Berger, *Ways of Seeing* (New York: Penguin, 1990).

[2] See Damon Johnston, "U.S. Hits Back Inspirations," *The Advertiser*, 22 September 2001, p. 7.

[3] See John Pomfret, "Chinese Working Overtime to Sew U.S. Flags", *Washington Post*, 20 September 2001, p. A14.

[4] See "Democracy: Who's She When She's at Home" in *The Algebra of Infinite Justice* (London: Flamingo, 2002), p. 235.

[5] See David E. Sanger, "Bin Laden Is Wanted in Attacks, 'Dead or Alive,' President Says", *New York Times*, 18 September 2001, p. A1; and John F. Burns, "10-Month Afghan Mystery: Is bin Laden Dead or Alive?", *New York Times*, 30 September 2002, p. A1.

[6] See the Associated Press database of those confirmed dead, reported dead or reported missing in the September 11th terrorist attacks (http://attacksvictims.ap.org/totals.asp).

[7] Quoted in Seymour M. Hersh, *The Price of Power: Kissinger in the Nixon White House* (New York: Summit Books, 1983), p. 265.

[8] See *Chile: The Other September 11*, eds. Pilar Aguilera and Ricardo Fredes (New York: Ocean Press, 2002); Amnesty International, "The Case of Augusto Pinochet" (http://www.amnestyusa.org/countries/chile/pinochet_case.html).

[9] Clifford Krauss, "Britain Arrests Pinochet to Face Charges by Spain", *New York Times*, 18 October 1998, p. 1: 1; National Security Archive, "Chile: 16,000 Secret U.S. Documents Declassified," Press Release, 13 November 2000 (http://www.gwu.edu/~nsarchiv/news/20001113/); and selected documents on the National Security Archive website (http://www.gwu.edu/~nsarchiv/news/20001113/#docs).

[10] Kissinger told this to Pinochet at a meeting of the Organization of American States in Santiago, Chile, on 8 June 1976. See Lucy Kosimar, "Kissinger Covered Up Chile Torture", *Observer*, 28 February 1999, p. 3.

[11] Among other histories, see Eduardo Galeano, *Open Veins of Latin America: Five Centuries of the Pillage of a Continent*, 2nd ed., trans. Cedric Belfrage (New York: Monthly Review Press, 1998); Noam Chomsky, *Turning the Tide: U.S. Intervention in Central America and the Struggle for Peace*, 2nd ed. (Boston: South End Press, 1985); Noam

Chomsky, *The Culture of Terrorism* (Boston: South End Press, 1983); and Gabriel Kolko, *Confronting the Third World: United States Foreign Policy, 1945–1980* (New York: Pantheon, 1988).

[12] In a public relations move, the SOA renamed itself the Western Hemisphere Institute for Security Cooperation (WHISC) on 17 January 2001. See Jack Nelson-Pallmeyer, *School of Assassins: Guns, Greed, and Globalization*, 2nd ed. (New York: Orbis Books, 2001); Michael Gormley, "Army School Faces Critics Who Call It Training Ground for Assassins", Associated Press, 2 May 1998; and School of the Americas Watch (http://www.soaw.org).

[13] On these interventions, see, among other sources, Noam Chomsky, *American Power and the New Mandarins*, 2nd ed. (New York: New Press, 2002); Noam Chomsky, *At War With Asia* (New York: Vintage Books, 1970); and Howard Zinn, *Vietnam: The Logic of Withdrawal*, 2nd ed. (Cambridge, Mass: South End Press, 2002).

[14] See Samih K. Farsoun and Christina E. Zacharia, *Palestine and the Palestinians* (Boulder, Colorado: Westview Press, 1997), p. 10.

[15] The Balfour Declaration is included in Farsoun and Zacharia, *Palestine and the Palestinians*, Appendix 2, p. 320.

[16] Quoted in Noam Chomsky, *Fateful Triangle: The United States, Israel, and the Palestinians*, 2nd ed. (Cambridge, Mass.: South End Press, 2000), p. 90.

[17] Quoted in Editorial, "Scurrying Towards Bethlehem", *New Left Review* 10, 2nd series (July/August 2001), p. 9, n. 5.

[18] Quoted in Farsoun and Zacharia, *Palestine and the Palestinians*, pp. 10 and 243.

[19] Ibid, pp. 111 and 123.

[20] Ibid, p. 116.

[21] See Chomsky, *Fateful Triangle*, pp. 103–7, 118–32, and 156–60.

[22] From 1987 to 2002 alone, more than 2,000 Palestinians have been killed. See B'Tselem (The Israeli Information Center for Human Rights in the Occupied Territories), "Palestinians Killed in the Occupied Territories", Table (http://www.btselem.org/English/Statistics/Total_Casualties.asp).

[23] See Naseer H. Aruri, *Dishonest Broker: The United States, Israel, and the Palestinians* (Cambridge, Mass.: South End Press, forthcoming); Noam Chomsky, *World Orders Old and New*, 2nd ed. (New York: Columbia University Press, 1996).

[24] See Nick Anderson, "House Panel Increases Aid for Israel, Palestinians", *Los Angeles Times*, 10 May 2002, p. A1; Aruri, *Dishonest Broker*, Appendix 1 and Appendix 2; and Anthony Arnove and Ahmed Shawki, "Foreword", *The Struggle for Palestine*, ed. Lance Selfa (Chicago: Haymarket Books, 2002), p. xxv.

[25] Article 27 of the Charter of the Islamic Resistance Movement (Hamas), quoted in Farsoun and Zacharia, *Palestine and the Palestinians*, Appendix 13, p. 339.

[26] George W. Bush, "Text of Bush's Speech: 'It Is Iraq Against the World'", *Los Angeles Times*, 12 September 1990, p. A7.

[27] See Glenn Frankel, "Iraq Long Avoided Censure on Rights", *Washington Post*, 22 September 1990, p. A1.

[28] See Christopher Dickey and Evan Thomas, "How Saddam Happened", *Newsweek*, 23 September 2002, pp. 35–7.

[29] See Anthony Arnove, Introduction, *Iraq Under Siege: The Deadly Impact of Sanctions and War*, 2nd ed., ed. Anthony Arnove (Cambridge, Mass.: South End Press; London: Pluto Press, 2002), p. 20.

[30] See Arnove, *Iraq Under Siege*, pp. 221–2.

[31] See Arnove, *Iraq Under Siege*, pp. 17, 205.

[32] See Thomas J. Nagy, "The Secret Behind the Sanctions: How the US Intentionally Destroyed Iraq's Water Supply", *The Progressive* 65: 9 (September 2001).

[33] See Arnove, *Iraq Under Siege*, pp. 121 and 185–203. See also Nicholas D. Kristof, "The Stones of Baghdad," *New York Times*, 4 October 2002, p. A27.

[34] Leslie Stahl, "Punishing Saddam," produced by Catherine Olian, CBS, *60 Minutes*, 12 May 1996.

[35] Elisabeth Bumiller, "Bush Aides Set Strategy to Sell Policy on Iraq", *New York Times*, 7 September 2002, p. A1.

[36] Richard Perle, "Why the West Must Strike First Against Saddam Hussein", *Daily Telegraph* (London), 9 August 2002, p. 22.

[37] See Alan Simpson and Glen Rangwala, "The Dishonest Case for a War on Iraq", 27 September 2002 (http://www.traprockpeace.org/counter-dossier.html) and Glen Rangwala, "Notes Further to the Counter-Dossier", 29 September 2002 (http://www.traprockpeace.org/counter-dossier.html#notes).

[38] George Bush, "Bush's remarks on U.S. Military Strikes in Afghanistan", *New York Times*, 8 October 2001, p. B6.

[39] See Paul Watson, "Afghanistan Aims to Revive Pipeline Plans", *Los Angeles Times*, 30 May 2002, p. A1; Ilene R. Prusher, Scott Baldauf and Edward Girardet, "Afghan Power Brokers," *Christian Science Monitor*, 10 June 2002, p. 1.

[40] See Lisa Fingeret et al., "Markets Worry That Conflict Could Spread in Area That Holds Two-Thirds of World Reserves", *Financial Times* (London), 2 April 2002, p. 1.

[41] Thomas L. Friedman, "Craziness Pays", *New York Times*, 24 February 1998, p. A21.

[42] Thomas L. Friedman, *The Lexus and the Olive Tree: Understanding Globalization* (New York: Farrar, Strauss & Giroux, 1999), p. 373.

[43] Statistics from Joseph E. Stiglitz, *Globalization and Its Discontents* (New York and London: W. W. Norton, 2002), p. 5; Noam Chomsky, *Rogue States: The Rule of Law in World Affairs* (Cambridge, Mass.: South End Press, 2000), p. 214; and Noreena Hertz, "Why Consumer Power Is Not Enough", *New Statesman*, 30 April 2001.

[44] Among the many treaties and international agreements the United States has not signed, ignores, violates or has broken are: UN International Covenant on Economic, Social and Cultural Rights (1966); the UN Convention on the Rights of the Child (CRC); the UN Convention on the Elimination of All Forms of Discrimination Against Women (CEDAW); agreements setting the jurisdiction for the International Criminal Court (ICC); the 1972 Anti-Ballistic Missile Treaty with Russia; the Comprehensive Test Ban Treaty (CTBT); and the Kyoto Protocol regulating greenhouse gas emissions.

[45] See David Cole and James X. Dempsey, *Terrorism and the Constitution: Sacrificing Civil Liberties in the Name of National Security* (New York: New Press, 2002).

[46] Luke Harding, "Elusive Mullah Omar 'Back in Afghanistan'", *Guardian* (London), 30 August 2002, p. 12.

[47] See Human Rights Watch, "Opportunism in the Face of Tragedy: Repression in the Name of Anti-Terrorism" (http://www.hrw.org/campaigns/september11/opportunismwatch.htm).

[48] Secretary of Defense Donald Rumsfield, Special Defense Briefing,'Developments Concerning Attacks on the Pentagon and the World Trade Center Last Week', Federal News Service, 20 September 2001).

the loneliness of noam chomsky

[1] R. W. Apple, Jr., "Bush Appears in Trouble Despite Two Big Advantages", *New York Times*, 4 August 1988, p. A1. Bush made this remark in refusing to apologize for the shooting down of an Iranian passenger plane, killing 290 passengers. See Lewis Lapham, *Theater of War* (New York: New Press, 2002), p. 126.

[2] Chomsky would be the first to point out that other pioneering media analysts include his frequent co-author Edward Herman, Ben Bagdikian (whose 1983 classic *The Media Monopoly* recounts the suppression of Chomsky and Herman's *Counter-Revolutionary Violence*) and Herbert Schiller.

[3] Paul Betts, "Ciampi Calls for Review of Media Laws," *Financial Times* (London), 24 July 2002, p. 8. For an overview of Berlusconi's holdings, see Ketupa.net Media Profiles: http://www.ketupa.net/berlusconi1.htm.

[4] See Sabin Russell, "U.S. Push for Cheap Cipro Haunts AIDS Drug Dispute", *San Francisco Chronicle*, 8 November 2001, p. A13; Frank Swoboda and Martha McNeil Hamilton, "Congress Passes $15 Billion Airline Bailout", *Washington Post*, 22 September 2001, p. A1.

[5] President George W. Bush Jr., "President Bush's Address on Terrorism Before a Joint Meeting of Congress", *New York Times*, 21 September 2001, p. B4.

[6] Dan Eggen, "Ashcroft Invokes Religion In U.S. War on Terrorism", *Washington Post*, 20 February 2002, p. A2.

[7] President George W. Bush Jr., "Bush's Remarks on U.S. Military Strikes in Afghanistan", *New York Times*, 8 October 2001, p. B6.

[8] President George W. Bush Jr., Remarks at FBI Headquarters, Washington, D.C., 10 October 2001, Federal Document Clearinghouse.

[9] See Howard Zinn, *A People's History of the United States: 1492–Present*, 20th anniversary edition (New York: HarperCollins, 2001).

[10] Bob Marley and N. G. Williams (a.k.a. King Sporty), "Buffalo Soldier".

[11] Noam Chomsky, "The Manufacture of Consent", in *The Chomsky Reader*, ed. James Peck (New York: Pantheon, 1987), pp. 121–2.

[12] See Jim Miller, "Report From the Inferno", *Newsweek*, 7 September 1981, p. 72, Review of Committee for the Compilation of Materials on Damage Caused by the Atomic Bombs in Hiroshima and Nagasaki, *Hiroshima and Nagasaki: The Physical, Medical, and Social Effects of the Atomic Bombings* (New York: Basic, 1981).

[13] David E. Sanger, "Bush to Formalize a Defense Policy of Hitting First", *New York Times*, 17 June 2002, p. A1; David E. Sanger, "Bush Renews Pledge to Strike First to Counter Terror Threats," *New York Times*, 20 July 2002, p. A3. See also *The National Security Strategy of the United States of America*, 20 September 2002: http://www.whitehouse.gov/nsc/nss.html.

[14] See Terence O'Malley, "The Afghan Memory Holds Little Room for Trust in US", *Irish Times*, 15 October 2001, p. 16.

[15] See Anthony Arnove, ed., *Iraq Under Siege: The Deadly Impact of Sanctions and War*, 2nd ed. (Cambridge, Mass.: South End Press; London: Pluto Press, 2002).

[16] See Noam Chomsky, "Memories", review of *In Retrospect* by Robert McNamara (New York: Times Books, 1995), in *Z* magazine (July–August 1995). Available online at http://www.zmag.org/.

[17] "Myth and Reality in Bloody Battle for the Skies", *Guardian* (London), 13 October 1998, p. 15.

[18] Bill Keller, "Moscow Says Afghan Role Was Illegal and Immoral", *New York Times*, 24 October 1989, p. A1.

[19] Noam Chomsky, "Afghanistan and South Vietnam", in *The Chomsky Reader*, ed. Peck, p. 225.

[20] Samuel P. Huntington, "The Bases of Accommodation", *Foreign Affairs* 46: 4 (1968): 642–56. Quoted in Noam Chomsky, *At War with Asia* (New York: Vintage Books, 1970), p. 87.

[21] Samuel P. Huntington, "The Clash of Civilizations?", *Foreign Affairs* 72: 3 (Summer 1993), pp. 22–49.

[22] Huntington, "The Bases of Accommodation". Quoted in Chomsky, *At War with Asia*, p. 87.

[23] T. D. Allman, "The Blind Bombers", *Far Eastern Economic Review* 75: 5 (29 January 1972), pp. 18–20. Quoted in Noam Chomsky, *For Reasons of State* (New York: New Press, 2003), p. 72.

[24] Chomsky, *For Reasons of State*, p. 72; Chomsky, *At War with Asia*, p. 87; and Lapham, *Theater of War*, p. 145.

[25] T. D. Allman, "The War in Laos: Plain Facts," *Far Eastern Economic Review* 75: 2 (8 January 1972), p. 16. Quoted in Chomsky, *For Reasons of State*, pp. 173–4.

[26] Chomsky, *For Reasons of State*, p. 18. See also Noam Chomsky, "The Pentagon Papers as Propaganda and as History", in Noam Chomsky and Howard Zinn, ed., *The Pentagon Papers: The Defense Department History of United States Decisionmaking on Vietnam: The Senator Gravel Edition: Critical Essays* (Boston: Beacon Press, 1971–2), vol. 5, pp. 79–201.

[27] Chomsky, *For Reasons of State*, pp. 67 and 70.

[28] William Pfaff, *Condemned to Freedom: The Breakdown of Liberal Society* (New York: Random House, 1971), pp. 75–7. Quoted in Chomsky, *For Reasons of State*, p. 94.

[29] Pfaff, *Condemned to Freedom*, pp. 75–7. Chomsky, *For Reasons of State*, pp. 94–5.

[30] *The Pentagon Papers*, vol. 4, p. 43. Quoted in Chomsky, *For Reasons of State*, p. 67.

[31] Philip Jones Griffiths, *Vietnam Inc.*, 2nd ed. (New York: Phaidon, 2001). First edition quoted in Chomsky, *For Reasons of State*, pp. 3–4.

[32] Noam Chomsky, interview with James Peck, in *The Chomsky Reader*, ed. Peck, p. 14.

confronting empire

[1] See Ranjit Devraj, "Asia's 'Outcast' Hurt By Globalization", Inter Press Service, 6 January 2003; Statesman News Service, "Farm Suicide Heat on Jaya", *The Statesman* (India), 9 January 2003; and "'Govt. Policies Driving Farmers to Suicide'", *The Times of India*, 4 February 2002.

[2] See "Govt.'s Food Policy Gets a Reality Check from States", *Indian Express*, 11 January 2003; and Parul Chandra, "Victims Speak of Hunger, Starvation Across Country", *The Times of India*, 11 January 2003.

[3] See "Democracy: Who Is She When She's at Home?". See also Pankaj Mishra, "The Other Face of Fanaticism", *New York Times*, 2 February 2003, p. 6: 42–6; and Concerned Citizens Tribunal, *Crime Against Humanity: An Inquiry Into the Carnage of Gujarat*, 2 vols (Mumbai, India: Citizens for Justice and Peace, 2002).

[4] See Edward Luce, "Gujarat Win Likely to Embolden Hindu Right", *Financial Times* (London), 16 December 2002, p. 8.

[5] See Oscar Olivera, "The War Over Water in Cochabamba, Bolivia", "Services for All?", trans. Florencia Belvedere, presented at Municipal Services Project (MSP) Conference, South Africa, 15–18

May 2002, http://qsilver.queensu.ca/~mspadmin/pages/Conferences/
Services/Olivera.htm.

6 See Tom Lewis, "Contagion in Latin America", *International Socialist Review* 24 (July–August 2002).

7 See Julian Borger and Alex Bellos, "US 'Gave the Nod' to Venezuelan Coup", *Guardian* (London), 17 April 2002, p. 13.

8 See David Sharrock, "Thousands Protest in Buenos Aires as Economic Woes Persist", *The Times* (London), 21 December 2002, p. 18.

9 See Mary McGrory, " 'A River of Peaceful People,' " *Washington Post*, 23 January 2003, p. A21.